CW00517656

Celtic The Invincibles 2016-17

Celtic The Invincibles 2016-17
The Story Of A Remarkable Season
David Potter

First Published in Great Britain in 2017 by DB Publishing,
an imprint of JMD Media Ltd

© David Potter, 2017

All Rights Reserved. No part of this publication may be reproduced, stored in
a retrieval system, or transmitted in any form, or by any means, electronic,
mechanical, photocopying, recording or otherwise without the prior permission
in writing of the copyright holders, nor be otherwise circulated in any form
or binding or cover other than in which it is published and without a similar
condition being imposed on the subsequent publisher.

ISBN 978-1-78091-559-3

Printed and bound in the UK

CONTENTS

ACKNOWLEDGEMENTS

The chronicling of this remarkable season would not have been possible without the help and encouragement of loads of people.

The book is basically all about the Joseph Rafferty Celtic Supporters Club of Kirkcaldy, with whom I travel to most home games and quite a few away games. I am grateful to the many people on the bus with whom I discuss, animatedly but respectfully, the game in detail. Celtic means so much to so many people, and the passion for the football club which wears green and white jerseys never fails to amaze me. People like Youssuf, Rocco, Kai, Stephen, Joe, Chick, Ryan, Peter, Jim and many others whom I am insulting by failing to name (but there are so many of them!) have given me so much insight into what it means to be part of Celtic.

There are others whom I talk to in and around the ground, or even in the street. Celtic means so much to so many people. I hope they enjoy this book.

I would like to thank Eric McCowat for his help with the photographs, and Dan Coxon and Steve Caron for their help in the production of the book.

David Potter, July 2017

CHAPTER **ONE**
RONNIE DEILA – MANAGER OF CELTIC 2014–16

It remains difficult to assess the contribution to Celtic of Ronnie Deila. He was Manager for two years. In those two years, he won the Scottish Premier League two times, and thus remains the only Celtic Manager (leaving aside Brendan Rodgers, whose time is not yet complete at Celtic Park) with a 100 per cent record in this respect. In both years, he won the League handsomely and with loads of time to spare, and the historian in the distant future will look back on this with puzzlement. He also, in 2015, won the Scottish League Cup. He brought players like Stuart Armstrong and Dedryck Boyata to the club and played a part in the development of Kieran Tierney. He introduced the 'Ronnie Roar' at the end of a successful game in which he punched the air with his left hand, and there was a certain rapport between him and the support. Why, then, did the likeable Norwegian leave the club?

He arrived in summer 2014, after the not-really-all-that-well-explained departure of Neil Lennon. Lennon, we were told, left because he felt that the club lacked ambition. If there was anything in that, those who were looking for more ambition could hardly have been impressed by the Norwegian from a club called Stromgodset. Frankly, no one had ever heard of him, and there was the widespread belief that he was only there because he was cheap and easy to pay. He did not get off to the best of starts, as Celtic, playing their home games at Murrayfield because Celtic Park was being used for the 2014 Commonweath Games, departed the Champions League twice in odd circumstances, after Legia Warsaw fielded an illegal player! Legia were deposed and Celtic given another chance, but they still lost, this time at Parkhead, to Maribor of Slovenia. It was not the best of starts.

The word 'uninspired' is often used of Ronnie Deila, but the reason for his departure probably lies in his failure to get the club into the sectional stage of the European Champions League. Repeated failures to make any real impact on Europe from a succession of Managers sits ill with the Celtic fans, some of whom recalled 1967 – although, heaven knows, there has only been the occasional success to boast of since, and an awful lot of misery. The talk of the Croesus-type wealth of the Champions League, and indeed the English Premiership, was only a partial reason for this failure, and did not explain how we could not get past teams like Malmo and Maribor. Granted, there were a few moments in the Europa League – not least a creditable performance against Inter Milan – but no sustained success, and Deila's failure to establish a club with such a massive fan base as a thriving European concern counted very much against him.

He had little luck with some of his players. There was probably little he could have done to preserve Virgil Van Dijk in a green and white jersey, but Stefan Johansen, a very talented midfielder who had been so good in 2014/15, let him down badly in 2015/16, struggling with injury, form and occasionally (as it seemed to the cynical) commitment, but worse was the loss for a large part of the 2015/16 season of Scott Brown. Stuart Armstrong, Gary Mackay-Steven and Tom Rogic were adequate in midfield, but the loss of 'Broonie' was significant.

In addition to that, Ronnie had three Cup semi-finals at Hampden in which luck was not on his side. In April 2015, Celtic went down to Inverness Caledonian Thistle in a game always to be remembered for refereeing decisions. This was the semi-final of the Scottish Cup of 2015 – the Scottish League Cup was already comfortably in the bag – when Celtic, already a goal up, were denied another which also might have resulted in a red card being given to an Inverness player, who, photographic evidence proved, used an arm. The decision was clearly wrong, raised a few questions about referee Steven McLean and in particular about the efficacy of the two extra referees behind the goal, but it was not the game changer. The game changer was when Craig Gordon was sent off and a penalty awarded against Celtic in that draconian rule of 'denying a goal scoring opportunity'.

The game was hard to take and cost us the treble in 2015, but at this stage in April 2015, with the League Cup won and the League to be clinched in early May, feelings about Ronnie were still sympathetic. After all, two out of three is not all that bad, and the lost competition did a certain amount to gratify the Celtic paranoia of 'the world is against us'. The *world* really wasn't against us, however, because pundits and press agreed that Celtic had been ill done by. It was, however, particularly annoying to see Inverness lift the Scottish Cup in the final against Falkirk, a side now more beloved of the Parkhead faithful than had been the case of late, particularly as Peter Grant's son now played for them. Inverness thus joined the ranks of Dumbarton, St Bernard's, Dundee, Partick Thistle, Morton, Airdrie, East Fife and St Johnstone, teams who had won the Scottish Cup once and only once.

So Ronnie was still in the good books of the supporters in summer 2015, but that soon changed after the disastrous European campaign. Malmo of Sweden knocked us out, yet in the first leg at Celtic Park, until Malmo had scored a late goal to make the score 3–2 instead of 3–1, Celtic had looked comfortable. But at Malmo, Celtic went down 0–2. One of the goals was a very unlucky own goal conceded by Dedryck Boyata, but no one could deny that this was a very poor performance from Celtic, and richly did everyone deserve the verdict of the Green Brigade the following Saturday when a banner was unfurled saying 'Gutless in Malmo, Clueless in the Board Room', a fairly obvious dig at the lack of perceived investment in the club. Some newspapers used words like 'downsizing'.

The Europa League which followed this exit was an acute embarrassment, as the team failed to register a single victory against Fenerbahce, Molde or Ajax. Effie Ambrose gave away a howler of a goal against Fenerbahce, some bawheids picked fights in Amsterdam and worse of all, Kris Commons was seen to throw a rather public tantrum when he was substituted in the rain against Molde. Granted, Kris had not been having a good game, but he still remained Celtic's best hope, and his ire was directed mainly at John Collins, Ronnie Deila's assistant. The fans sided with Commons, but his subsequent appearances for the club were severely limited. By the end of this European campaign, Celtic were disorganised, and frankly, the fans did not really seem interested. Attendances were poor for European games and Ronnie never really recovered.

'Bad luck' is sometimes overused and inaccurately employed to justify incompetence and bad decision making, but even Deila's fiercest critics would have to concede that there was an element of misfortune about the semi-final exits in both Cup competitions in 2016. The Scottish League Cup semi-final at the end of January against Ross County saw Celtic go ahead in the first minute, but then the over-zealous refereeing of Craig Thomson awarded a penalty kick to Ross County and a red card to Efe Ambrose when the contact was minimal, and the initiative passed to the Staggies. As is often the case with people in difficulties in their life, a lifeline was offered in the shape of another penalty, but Leigh Griffiths missed it! Hard luck, but then again, many supporters argued that 'Celtic', 'hard luck' and 'Ross County' should never have to be used in the same sentence when we are talking about a small Highland team whose town's entire population could fit with comfort into the Jock Stein Stand!

This was bad, and made a great deal worse when we lost at Pittodrie on the following Wednesday in the League, thereby loosening, to a certain extent and only temporarily, our previously firm grip on the Scottish League, as the media began to chortle about 'there's now a challenger' and 'Celtic won't get it all their own way this season'. The big disaster of the season, however, was the losing of the Scottish Cup semi-final replay to Rangers (still only a Championship club) in April. It needed a penalty shoot-out – a form of the game in which Celtic have seldom excelled – but Celtic should have won in the 90 minutes. They chose to play very poorly, and failed to win. Defeats from Rangers usually have consequences. Apart from anything else, it meant that there would be no Scottish Cup Final appearance for Celtic. The knives were now out for Ronnie, whose departure was announced a few days later, even though Celtic had by now more or less won the League! He would be allowed to stay there to see out the campaign.

The form in the League had been pedestrian and plodding rather than spectacular. Two defeats at Pittodrie might have put the title in jeopardy but Aberdeen seemed to lack conviction on occasion, notably on Saturday, 19 March. Celtic were struggling and Aberdeen were within touching distance. Celtic were playing in the lunchtime kick-off game at Kilmarnock at Rugby Park, and the game was heading for a goalless draw (which would really have put the wind up Celtic and their anxious fans) until Tommy Rogic struck late from a distance. However impressed they may have been by the goal, the fans, who until the goal had been muttering and mutinous, exulted in the three points rather than the performance of the team.

One could, however, argue that it was Tommy Rogic who (temporarily, at any rate) saved Deila and won the Scottish League into the bargain. A hundred and fifty miles away at Pittodrie, Aberdeen had clearly been watching the game on the TV, with the supporters in all the pubs on Union Street and King Street enlivened by Celtic's struggling performance, as indeed were the players and the management. But Aberdeen were clearly upset by Tommy's late spectacular winner and went out to play their own game a little depressed. As is the way of the world, they blew up against Motherwell and lost!

The title was won for the 47th time, appropriately enough, against Aberdeen at Parkhead on 8 May, and Celtic supporters sang the praises of Ronnie Deila, who did a few 'Ronnie Roars' to the Green Brigade and everyone else, then turned their attention to discussing who his replacement was going to be, and showed their affection to Hibs for the Scottish Cup Final. They were not disappointed, for the Easter Road men, managed by ex-Celtic Alan Stubbs and with Anthony Stokes and Liam Henderson on board, beat Rangers in a thrilling final to win the Scottish Cup for the first time since the Boer War in 1902!

Thus ended 2015/16. The League had been won (and won well) but nothing else. This was not considered good enough, particularly when critics pointed out that there had been no Rangers since 2012 to trouble us. Nevertheless, some credit was deserved for Deila and his men, and the general opinion was that the team had many fine players, but needed a few more, and this time there really did have to be a challenge made for Europe. All these things were discussed when the game of 'guess the new Manager' was played by fans and by pundits, most of whom got it wrong!

It is often said that once the Manager 'loses the dressing room', he loses his job. No one knows what went on in that inner sanctum where, quite rightly, 'whatever happens in the dressing room stays there', but there was little doubt that Ronnie had lost the support from an early stage of this season, possibly as early as August when we failed to make it to the Champions League. The vitriol hurled at the likeable Norwegian was sometimes unwarranted and unfair, but there could be little doubt that the team, League Champions or not, were far from pleasing the customers as attendances dropped with loads of empty seats visible, and threats being made not to renew season tickets.

Ronnie had laid great stress on fitness, with much said about diet etcetera. It may be that he went too far down this road and antagonised a few players, whose form slumped in 2016. Certainly, there were several games at Celtic Park where there seemed to be a lack of 'drive' about the team, and the rather obvious under-employment of Kris Commons was a factor which caused distress. But whatever caused the disappointing performances, it is clear that the Manager must at all times take the blame for it. The Manager personifies the team in a way. If the team is brilliant, so is the Manager. If the team is mediocre, so is the Manager. Celtic supporters considered their team to be 'mediocre', and the Manager had to go, although one wonders what might have happened if the penalty shoot-out against Rangers had gone the other way.

While one sometimes deplores the cries of those who are 'not coming back', particularly after they used to sing a song about being 'faithful through and through', one has to realise that there is something endemically Celtic about all this. Celtic supporters are, almost by definition, rebels, and this has a good side as well. It means that we will never be short-changed. It means that at every point, the Directorate of the club will have to keep looking over their shoulders at the support, and make sure that they are happy.

One of the salient factors historically, however, is that sometimes the Celtic support are not noisy or nasty enough. They can be too docile. The horrible years from 1958–64 saw plenty of moaning, but only really one demonstration against the Kelly regime (in August 1963, after a terrible game against Queen of the South) and never any concerted movement to say, 'Enough is enough!'

until winter 1964/65 when the support eventually forced the hand of Bob Kelly. Similarly, in the early 1990s, we stoically put up with far too much from the same family dynasty until the last straws of early 1994, and even that was with considerable help from the Bank! Maybe, therefore, it was a good thing that the support in 2016 turned on the management after only two years. We must never put up with second best. By the same token, surely the greatest achievement of Brendan Rodgers all through season 2016/17 was that he managed to keep the supporters happy!

But to return to summer 2016, there never seemed to be any lack of journalists willing to make a fool of themselves by stating categorically in something called an 'exclusive' that Davie Moyes or Neil Lennon or anyone else one cared to name would be appointed Celtic's Manager today. Aye, it's 'exclusive' okay, because they just made it up! Amazingly, they still manage to retain some sort of credibility! But Celtic handled this one well, refused to appoint the man that the press told them to, interviewed more than six candidates according to Dermott Desmond, and on Friday, 20 May announced that Brendan Rodgers was to be the new Manager.

The day of 20 May was significant. It was early enough to allow the new Manager to make a few new signings, and the fact that it was the day before the Scottish Cup Final meant that it knocked Rangers off the headlines (an old Jock Stein trick, that one!), and that the talk of the steamie and everywhere else in Scottish football was the small dapper figure of Brendan Rodgers. Who was he?

CHAPTER **TWO**
BRENDAN RODGERS

Brendan Rodgers' reign as Manager of Liverpool never really survived the horrendous events of the evening of Monday, 5 May 2014. Liverpool were challenging hard for the Premiership. Their supporters were all too aware that they had never been able to call themselves Champions of England since 1990 and they had, therefore, never won the Premiership (established in 1993) at all. They had allowed themselves to be overwhelmed by Manchester United in a way that Celtic supporters of the early 1960s and of the 1990s would identify with – the simple idea that they were not allowed to win, and that the rule of Manchester United (and to a lesser extent Arsenal, Chelsea and Manchester City) was somehow pre-ordained. True, under a succession of Managers, they had had their successes in other competitions and indeed Europe, but the failure to be called Champions of England for more than two decades was the thing that hurt the most.

Brendan Rodgers.

Rodgers had been brought from Swansea (where he had been more than a reasonable success) to do just that, namely to win the English Premiership, and as the 2013/14 season was approaching its climax, Liverpool were locked in a titanic struggle with Manchester City. Liverpool had impressed in the early spring with eleven games won on the trot, and indeed they seemed irresistible as they were several points clear at one point. But a bad defensive error by that committed Liverpudlian Steven Gerrard against Chelsea on 27 April lost them the initiative, and then Manchester City came to the boil just at the wrong time for Brendan Rodgers.

But now things seemed to be going Liverpool's way again, with a very convincing performance against Crystal Palace at Selhurst Park this Bank Holiday Monday evening of 5 May. They were 3–0 up and playing like champions. They would be three points ahead of Manchester City, who had two games left, whereas Liverpool had only one game – a home fixture against the perpetually disappointing Newcastle United. Rodgers was aware, however, that City had a better goal difference, and he was keen to score more goals to reduce that leeway. The Liverpool fans who had travelled to London that night were confident and bubbly, singing the praises of Brendan Rodgers, for their team were playing well, and at long last there was a chance that Liverpool would once again be Champions of England. When Kenny Dalglish played for Liverpool, that seemed to happen more or less every year, but the dominance of Alex Ferguson and his Red Devils had been hard to take for the men with the horrendous Scouse accents, surely the worst and most cacophonic of them all.

What happened next is well documented on YouTube. Liverpool, in those last 11 minutes, managed to concede three goals to a middle-of-the-table but distinctly ordinary Crystal Palace in an astonishing way. Your writer recalls driving home from Edinburgh to Fife that evening and listening to the radio commentary on the excellent Radio 5. On the outskirts of Edinburgh, it was 3–0; by the Forth Bridge it was 3–3, with the commentators talking about a disaster of monumental proportions and saying that unless Manchester City blew up equally spectacularly, the title was theirs.

In this, they were proved correct. Celtic supporters, as a rule, have little love for Liverpool. There was an old score way back in 1966 when a good Lennox goal was ruled out for offside, and there was a continuing and long-lasting resentment of Kenny Dalglish doing so well for the Merseysiders when he could have been doing it for Celtic. So one would have to admit to a certain amount of *Schadenfreude* at their misery. Nevertheless, as a fellow football supporter one could understand the feelings of the Liverpool fans that night. A 'blowing up' is always hard to accept – we could recall with vivid clarity Motherwell in 2005 and Inverness in 2011, when SPLs were thrown away – and Liverpool fans were angry, although that emotion came later. There were first the stages of shock, numbness and disbelief to be worked through.

The dressing room being the sanctuary that it is, we will not know whether Rodgers 'lost the dressing room' that night. What is certain is that he definitely lost the support. Radio phone-ins for the next few days seemed to consist of nothing other than a long line of miserable, self-pitying Scouse voices in that distinctly unattractive accent of theirs, moaning about their lot and having a pop at Brendan Rodgers. These were interspersed with the gloating Evertonians and Manchester City supporters who now scented the League title. The real problem, as we all knew, however, was Manchester United, and the growing inferiority complex which Rodgers had not reversed.

The main thrust of the callers seemed to be that he should have strengthened the defence both in the long-term sense and also on that fateful night at Selhurst Park, when he was accused of going for more goals and leaving the back door open. A lot of that criticism was unfair. The same people would have been the first to say that it was a mistake to settle for a 3–0 win when more goals were required, and indeed possible, but in their grief and misery, the Liverpool supporters had to find some target, and Brendan Rodgers was in their sights.

Rodgers never really recovered at Anfield from this debacle. He retained his popularity with the owners, who extended his contract, but he never really won back the hearts of the fans. His personal life caused him problems as well but he stayed on as Manager for another year, in which Liverpool were 'all right, but nothing spectacular' and never really in contention for any of the trophies. They played good football and were frequently praised on *Match of the Day*, but the fact that they didn't win anything meant that the likeable Rodgers was the first Liverpool Manager since before Bill Shankly to have gone three seasons without winning a trophy. This sat ill with Liverpool. 'All right' is not really good enough for a team with the Shankly/Dalglish pedigree. Like the supporters of all great clubs, Celtic included, silverware is the lifeblood. They need to win.

Rodgers' sacking in October 2015 came as no great surprise to a world that looked upon the hiring and firing of Managers as an everyday, mundane occurrence. Form had been poor, and there had been a particular annoying tendency for the team to get ahead, then fail to get another goal with the inevitable then happening at the other end. It is probably fanciful to suggest, as some have done, that the players played their part in getting the Manager sacked. Everyone, however, recalled the events of 5 May 2014, and how different things might have been if they had won that night. That match, 5 May, was undeniably the reason for his sacking – even though it was a 'delayed action' sacking.

Nevertheless, Rodgers was hardly a failure either, and as he withdrew to lick his wounds and face the future, he reckoned that he had learned a great deal from his years in the game. Indeed he had. He had noted a few good players, and he would remember them. He fully intended to return to the game, but he could hardly have anticipated the dramatic turnaround of his fortunes in nine months' time.

The main perception among Celtic supporters on 20 May 2016 was that at last Celtic had 'gone big' when they brought Brendan Rodgers to Celtic Park. Ronnie Deila had been seen in some ways as a return to the penny-pinching 'biscuit tin' economy of the Kelly era. The word 'downsizing' was thrown about by those who wanted to jeer at Celtic. Rodgers, on the other hand, had seen a bit of footballing life with Liverpool, and to a lesser extent with Swansea, and he'd had experience in Europe. Europe was, of course, the key thing, although there was also in 2016 the realisation that Rangers would be back in the Premier League.

So Brendan Rodgers was greeted with joy. It was described as a 'coup' in the newspapers, although supporters, in a sad comment about the teaching of French in Scottish schools, described it as a 'cowp'. Some were disappointed that Neil Lennon was not given a chance to come back, but then again, his departure in 2014 had been abrupt and still not satisfactorily explained. Davie Moyes, a man who had done very well at Everton but less well at Manchester United, before becoming in 2017 a total disaster at that graveyard of Managers, Sunderland, was in the frame for a spell, and there were the recurrent favourites of Roy Keane and Malky MacKay, but Brendan Rodgers seemed a good choice. Certainly, very soon after his appointment, he was seen talking to supporters. He was charming, well-dressed, smaller than most Managers – but who was he?

In his unveiling, seated between Peter Lawwell and Ian Bankier, he was careful to stress his love for the club and Lawwell used words like 'affinity and affection'. Brendan made everyone aware that he loved the club and knew all about the Lisbon Lions. He was pledged to continue the League dominance – the club had won five titles in a row – but he clearly had his eyes on the European scene. He said all the right things and he was clearly off on the right foot. He was soon introduced to the fans with Leigh Griffiths carrying out the League trophy. It was a fine piece of Celtic public relations. Things were definitely upbeat.

Brendan Rodgers was born on 26 January 1973 in Carnlough, County Antrim. Being born in that place at that time means that he cannot but have been aware of the awful time that Northern Ireland was going through with violence, bombings and assassinations, but Brendan is a bigot's nightmare, in that his parents had a mixed marriage. One was Catholic and the other Protestant, and they loved each other! Possibly for this reason, but also because of his general wisdom and common sense, he grew up to hate sectarianism, seeing for himself all the harm that it caused. He grew up with a love of football, and supported Sheffield Wednesday in England and Celtic in Scotland.

Born six years after Lisbon and with Jock Stein's side about to win their eighth successive League title (with a bit more of a struggle this year), Brendan was thus probably just too young to know much about the Ten Men winning the League in 1979, but he would have known all about the two great 'comeback' Cup Finals of 1985 and 1988 against Dundee United, the epic winning of the League with the help of Albert Kidd in 1986 and the Centenary Double of 1988. Sadly, too, he would have known all about the evil days of the early 1990s when the word 'finished' was used about Celtic, so apathetic and self-seeking were the Board of Directors who tamely allowed Rangers to win nine League Championships in a row before Nemesis, that goddess of Greek mythology who eventually punishes the wicked, appeared in 1994 to break the deleterious Kelly regime. She would return in 2012 to wreak an even more dreadful vengeance on the winners of 1994.

Naturally, Brendan played the game of football and managed the unlikely feat, if Wikipedia is to be believed, of playing at schoolboy International level for both Northern Ireland and the Republic of Ireland. His career began with Ballymena United, and then he was considered good enough to be signed on for Reading. Sadly, his playing career never really took off, for he had a problem with his knee, and in 1993 he decided reluctantly to give up the playing side of the game. This must have been a blow to the earnest young man who simply loved football, but it was an early introduction to the undeniable fact that football kicks one in the teeth now and again.

Such was Brendan's impressive ability in the coaching side of the game that he was appointed Director of the Reading Youth Academy, where he worked with a young Irishman called Jonny Hayes. Then, in 2004, he met no less a person than Jose Mourinho and was given a post similar to his Reading one at Chelsea, and later became Manager of the reserve side. He was then appointed Manager of Watford, and then he returned to Reading to be their Manager, but it would be fair to say that he did not distinguish himself in either post, and it was only when he was appointed to the job at Swansea City in summer 2010 that he really began to experience some kind of success.

Swansea City were a challenge. An underperforming club in a country that traditionally preferred rugby to football, and still does, Swansea were a bit of a sleeping giant with a support that needed to be energised. In the 2010/11 season they played in the Championship with the services of a player called Scott Sinclair, whom Rodgers clearly admired. They missed out on the automatic promotion spot, but in one of the highlights of Swansea's sad and disappointing history, at the end of May 2011, Swansea beat Reading 4–2 with a hat-trick from Scott Sinclair and became the first Welsh side to enter the Premiership.

The Premiership brought a great deal of money, of course, and a certain amount of exposure in the national media. It was confidently expected, even by some of Swansea's own supporters, that their return back down to the Championship would be immediate, but Rodgers was able, by his knowledge of the game and by not doing anything stupid, to earn his side a respectable place in the Premiership. They finished 11th out of 20, and finished the season by beating Liverpool. He won the award Manager of the Month in February 2012 and was given a new contract by his grateful employers. He had even defeated Celtic in a pre-season friendly!

Such success at a club with what was, by Premier League standards, a limited budget impressed everyone and Liverpool made their move in summer 2012. He was by no means a failure at Liverpool in his three and a bit years, but he was not a success either, and Liverpool fans, embittered by over twenty years of losing out to Manchester United, Chelsea and Arsenal in the Premier League, could not accept that. His success rate was almost exactly 50 per cent, something that would have been totally acceptable in any other club, but not Liverpool, and eventually a combination of some half-hearted players, perpetual moaning by fans and a certain disillusionment on the part of the Directors forced him out, the axe being employed, bizarrely, about an hour after a 1–1 draw with Everton in early October 2015, in a game which mirrored so much of Rodgers' career at Anfield – good, but not good enough.

In some ways, he was not the stereotype of a Manager. He was not flamboyant or extroverted like his successor at Anfield, Jurgen Klopp, and touchline brawls and altercations with the rival Manager or the referee were alien to him. He would not have relished a 'square go' with another Manager (as two Scottish Managers, with Celtic connections, who should have known a lot better offered each other allegedly in season 2016/17) and he was always seen to be very gentlemanly and courteous with his opposite number, a characteristic that he has laudably kept at Celtic Park. He was once, in December 2013, when with Liverpool, in trouble over comments he made about referee Lee Mason, who he felt should not have been given a Liverpool v. Manchester City game as he lived in Manchester. That was an aberration, and he was duly fined £8,000. He regretted having said that, but that of course was the year in which Manchester City pipped Liverpool to the Premiership title, and there were a few debatable decisions which went against Liverpool in that game.

Winter and Christmas 2015, after his sacking, were spent in quiet reflection by Brendan. He may have dabbled with the idea of giving up football altogether, he may have dabbled with the idea of becoming a pundit (on the few occasions when he appeared on radio or TV, he came across well as a quiet-spoken, restrained, knowledgeable character). He had amassed enough money, one assumes, to render unnecessary an immediate return to football, and who knows where his career was heading until the Celtic job became available. That was an offer that he could not refuse. Who could? He had loved Celtic when he was young, and normally one does not change. Indeed, it is not really a matter of individual choice.

On 20 May 2016, therefore, Brendan Rodgers joined the ranks of Willie Maley, Jimmy McStay, Jimmy McGrory, Jock Stein, Billy McNeill, David Hay, Billy McNeill (again), Liam Brady, Lou Macari, Tommy Burns, Wim Jansen, Jo Venglos, John Barnes, Kenny Dalglish, Martin O'Neill, Gordon Strachan, Tony Mowbray, Neil Lennon and Ronnie Deila. Some of these are legends – Maley, Stein without a doubt, and a strong case could be made for McNeill and O'Neill, others were not there for long enough to make a judgement, some – Venglos, Barnes and Mowbray – simply not up to the awesome demands of this job. How would he fit in?

Rodgers did have some advantages. His love of Celtic in his childhood meant that he knew what the club meant. He was not a hired mercenary. He would be well paid, but there was also an emotional investment as well. There was also the personal point that having been a Manager at a big club and having failed to lift a trophy, he really could not afford to fizzle out at Celtic, otherwise he would lose credibility. He had, of course, all the experience required. He had dealt with people like Sterling and Suarez, he had faced Ferguson, Wenger and Mourinho, he could handle the media and he was clearly very good at public relations. He seemed to tick all the boxes, and he had the necessary hunger.

His major disadvantage, as it appeared in May 2016, was that he had no experience of Scotland. Scotland may be a small country, much derided by know-alls in England and elsewhere, but it is incredibly complex and difficult for an outsider to come to terms with. Those who cry 'No opposition in Scotland' are delivering a great insult to the likes of Aberdeen, who work hard on a limited budget. Rangers, granted, had been out of the top Division for some time – but they were now back and Hearts were a team who always had great (sadly often unfulfilled) potential. In any case, no matter how poor the opposition, you still have to beat them!

But that was only half the problem. Every team in Scotland wanted to beat Celtic. Kilmarnock, Inverness and St Johnstone, for example, who often play dreadful games of football against each other in front of desperately poor crowds, nevertheless see the approach of Celtic as a Cup Final. Everything is put into it, the game is often on TV, and Celtic seldom find such games easy. Indeed, it is often illuminating if you have a pint with, say, a Motherwell supporter after a game with Celtic at Fir Park. A constant refrain will always be 'If only we could play like that every week...'

In addition, there were other 'Scottish' things to consider. Celtic had to know which pitches were good and which bad – television, for example, gives no indication of the pronounced cross-field slope at Motherwell, for you have to be there behind a goal to notice it – weather could often be dreadful and notoriously unpredictable, and there were tackles that Scottish referees might not allow and others that they would. All these things needed a certain amount of knowledge and experience of Scotland. This Rodgers did not have – yet it would not be a real problem, for he had with him men like Scott Brown and Craig Gordon who certainly did understand Scotland.

There was also – and Brendan would certainly have been aware of this – the less pleasant side of Scottish football, involving the less intelligent members of the other persuasions. One Celtic Manager in recent years has been physically attacked at Tynecastle – and the crowd cheered! – as well as being sent bullets in the post! Another had a Union Jack planted in his garden one night! Anyone coming to Scotland would have to reckon with this. Those of us not directly involved in this sort of nonsense can shake our heads at the failure of the Scottish educational system to eradicate this problem – although, God knows, they have tried! – and it is indeed the manifestation of the ignorant, lunatic fringe, but it is a problem nevertheless.

Brendan Rodgers, however, decided that he would take a chance.

CHAPTER **THREE**
GIBRALTAR AND RECOVERY

To say that Celtic and Brendan Rodgers simply had to qualify for the sectional stages of the European Champions League was stating the obvious. Credibility was at stake. It would be no easy task, for Celtic had three hurdles to overcome before they could be among the big boys again. It was a time of the year when football was not always the first thought that entered anyone's mind, and many of Celtic's Scottish players, at least, had no great experience of playing in the heat of a European summer. It also meant that Brendan Rodgers had no real time to analyse his squad. Naturally, he had followed the fortunes of the club before his appointment, but that was not the same thing as being Manager and making vital decisions. He had, however, as we will see, kept his eyes and ears wide open while watching English football.

The reason for the unconscionably early start was, of course, something called the co-efficient. It was a remarkable, mysterious, enigmatic, incomprehensible (even to most journalists) sort of a thing, but undeniably, Scotland's was not good enough. The reason for this was decades of Scottish underperformance in Europe by a variety of teams. There is little point in denying that, apart from the odd good, even brilliant performance against Manchester United or Barcelona, Celtic's record was a shocker. Teams like Legia Warsaw, Malmo, Molde and Maribor had beaten Celtic in recent years when they had no right to expect to do so, given the disparity in the clubs' budgets. And that was in recent years and before we go back to the grizzly horrors of longer ago, when teams like Neuchatel Xamax and Artmedia Bratislava had done the deed over us!

Opponents of Celtic in Scotland probably get fed up of us talking constantly of Lisbon and 1967. They probably have a point when they say that the achievement, brilliant and iconic though it was, is harped on about ad nauseam (at least as far as lovers of Rangers and Aberdeen are concerned). The snag is that, in some ways, 1967 covers up the shortcomings that have been so obvious over the past fifty years. Frankly, a team of Celtic's support should have done a great deal better in the years since 1967. One can, in this respect, point to a parallel with the 7–1 game of 1957. We went on about it so much, because there was so little else to be happy about in the subsequent years – we did, for example, go four years from 1960–64 without beating Rangers in a national competition, and in season 1963/4 we managed to lose five times to them. So it was with Celtic in Europe. The record was, frankly, a shocker.

Celtic supporters have a great taste for nostalgia. It must never be discouraged, for it is a truism that someone who does not know his past, has no future. Reminiscence, however, becomes more pronounced when the present team is not doing so well. It was surely time for Celtic to reassert themselves on the European stage which seemed to have left them so far behind. Maybe we couldn't really compete financially (given the ill division of wealth) with the super-bucks of Real Madrid and Manchester United, but we did have a duty to our supporters (and we have as many worldwide as anyone) and to our fine sense of history to re-establish Celtic as a credible European team.

If we can point to anything that we have done wrong, it is naïve defending. In Europe, marking simply has to be tight, and if there was ever any game which highlighted this facet of Celtic's play, it was surely that awful night in September 1989 when Dziekanowski scored four goals against Partisan Belgrade, but Celtic still lost! From 1980 until well into the twenty-first century, Celtic's European campaigns failed to pass Christmas, and it was all so predictable to read in the press on some Thursday morning in autumn that 'the back door had been left open' and Celtic were out on 'away goals'.

But to return to the wretched co-efficient, other Scottish teams were doing us no favours either. Rangers, of course, had been out of the picture since their demise in 2012, but other teams like Aberdeen, Dundee United, Hearts, Hibs, St Johnstone and Inverness Caledonian Thistle could be relied upon to not so much 'blow up' as 'fizzle out' against teams who in European terms did not even reach the rank of mediocre. The players of these foreign clubs often returned from this strange land called Scotland, unable to believe that the beautiful land of hills, bagpipes and tartan had once nurtured winners of the European Cup!

The irony was that in March and April, Scottish newspapers and radio programmes began to always tell you that this was a 'must win' game for somebody so that they could qualify for Europe, as if this was some kind of Eldorado. Dick Whittington got a disappointment when he reached London to discover that the streets of London were not paved with gold, but at least he was there for long enough to have a good look round. Scottish clubs, who had sometimes organised laps of honour for 'qualifying for Europe' in May, were usually defeated and disillusioned by the end of July and before the Scottish season even got started! 'Ah, but if you get third this year, you would qualify for Europe!' Grim reality often asked the question, 'So?'

Jokes about getting home before the postcards were prevalent every summer. On 23 June 2016, the British people in their wisdom (or lack of it) had voted to leave Europe. Scotland had voted to remain, but no one seemed to tell the football teams that! The pattern was depressingly familiar, as indeed were all the excuses which were trotted out regularly – 'it was too early', 'the refereeing was poor', 'it was too hot' – all these were simply excuses unconvincingly masking the fact that Scottish teams were simple naïve and failed to 'wise up' to what was required. They were far too late in bringing their players back from holiday for intensive training, they would regularly fail to finish teams off at home, they would travel unaware that the way their opponents played in Scotland would be radically different from the way they performed on their own home ground, a dodgy decision would be given by the referee at a crucial point, and in particular, they failed to understand the 'away goals' rule, and how to deal with it. And then they complained about not having enough money!

So, Brendan Rodgers was aware that he must not succumb to the Scottish disease of a spectacular collapse in Europe before the season even got going. The first game was to be played on Tuesday, 12 July (a date that is never exactly a favourite with Celtic supporters!) against a Gibraltar team called Lincoln Red

Imps, and the first leg was to be played in Gibraltar. Rodgers had four friendlies before then, all abroad against NK Celje, Sturm Graz, Olimpija Ljubljana and our old friends Maribor. Two were won and two were drawn, and the squad was given a reasonable run out in the traditional low-key start to the season, as the rest of the country enjoyed summer sunshine with Wimbledon, golf and cricket, and began to realise the implications of the vote to leave Europe.

And so it was the Victoria Stadium, Gibraltar where Celtic kicked off their 2016/17 season. It was a stadium shared (incredibly) by all the ten teams in the Gibraltar Premier League, which had been won by Lincoln Red Imps for the past fourteen years! (This makes ten in a row seem rather weak, does it not?) The ground was situated in Winston Churchill Avenue, the name of which says an awful lot about Gibraltar's relationship with the rest of the world. Excessively patriotic, imperialist and pro-British with excessive flauntings of Union Jacks and pictures of the Royal Family (not unlike Govan, perhaps, or Larkhall!) they are a quaint anachronism. In the days of Franco's evil dictatorship in Spain, one could perhaps sympathise, but things had changed and a new, more realistic and forward-looking relationship with Spain and Europe was surely required. But did someone mention 'Brexit'?

Rodgers' team for his first game was Gordon, Janko, Sviatchenko, Ambrose, Tierney, Brown, Bitton, Rogic, Christie, Dembele, Griffiths with Armstrong, Forrest and Ciftci coming on as substitutes. The heat was intense, but that hardly excuses such a substandard performance as a fellow called Lee Casciaro, who had also scored for Gibraltar against Scotland at Hampden in March 2015, scored the only goal of the game. Twice Leigh Griffiths hit the bar, but all this meant that the part-timers who were policemen, teachers and firemen in their day jobs had beaten Glasgow Celtic 1–0. The crowd of 1,500 could hardly believe it all, and it was perhaps a blessing that there was no great Celtic support in the crowd. It would not have been an enjoyable experience. Not even an away goal to cheer!

There was a certain overdrive in the media reaction. Phrases like 'the worst defeat in Celtic's history' and 'Europe's greatest ever upset' were trotted out for the benefit of the gullible, and it certainly was a wake-up call to Celtic and Rodgers, but a more sober analysis would suggest that the defeat was simply due to lack of match fitness in the first game of the season. We could also trot out the old ones about the pitch and the referee, but cynics also were not slow to suggest that the crowd and potential revenue at Parkhead for next week's second leg was not likely to suffer as a result of this game! In any case, if you are to lose a match, the first game of the season is surely the best time to do it. Nearly sixty other fixtures remained this season!

One wondered, however, what Moussa Dembele made of all this. It was, as it turned out, his 20th birthday, and he was playing his debut for Celtic. It was a fair bet that no one had heard of him when he signed for Celtic a couple of weeks before, but the young Frenchman had clearly impressed for Fulham, for whom he had scored fifteen goals. He had also done well for the various French youth teams. Clearly one of the benefits of Rodgers' enforced leisure after October 2015 had been that he had had plenty of time to study players like Dembele. This was a far from impressive debut for Moussa, however, and he was taken off and substituted. Welcome to Celtic!

Clearly, by the time the Gibraltarians came to Glasgow on the following Wednesday, Rodgers had had another think about his squad, and the 55,632 crowd saw the welcome introduction of Patrick Roberts and Callum McGregor. Roberts had been with Celtic on loan from Manchester City since the previous winter. He had impressed when he played with some very good games, but he was very much a one-footed player with his left foot far more effective than his right. McGregor was one of those players who realised that this season was going to make him or break him. Still a young lad, the problem was that he did not really seem to do enough for the club. He'd had his chance, but he had frequently seemed, under Ronnie Deila, to be unhappy or in the wrong position. This night would be a very important one for Callum.

One look at the Gibraltarians as they took the field before the huge crowd confirmed that, unless Celtic were very stupid or played very badly, they had little to fear. The crowd of 55,000 was not far short of twice the entire population of the Rock, and it was immediately clear that the Red Imps had seen nothing vaguely like this. When the hard, experienced men of Barcelona and Inter Milan have been known to confess fear at the awesome atmosphere of Celtic Park on a European night, what chance did the Gibraltar posties have?

In fact, the Imps played creditably and deserved their round of applause at the end of the game, but were swept aside in a six-minute spell in the first half. The League flag, won last year, was unfurled before the game and Celtic played like champions. Mikael Lustig had the honour of scoring the first goal, a curling left-foot shot into the Lisbon Lions end of the ground before Leigh Griffiths added another from the edge of the box, picking up a fine through ball from Patrick Roberts, and then Roberts himself hit a third after a fine one-two involving Callum McGregor.

And that was just about all there was to it, with the second half seeing Celtic playing some fine football, the Imps showing the occasional good touch and their goalkeeper having a stormer, but the result was in little doubt. The main element in the eyes of the supporters was relief at avoiding a humiliation, and one step had been taken towards the sectional stages of the Champions League, as all those who had talked with such glee about last week's result were served a rather large helping of humble pie. And those who had avidly read such trash could be told that they had removed the word 'gullible' from the English Dictionary! 'Eh, have they?'

The following night, Thursday, 21 July, saw Edinburgh 'doing the Scottish thing' and departing early from Europe. Hearts hinted at the dreadful season that they were about to inflict on their supporters by losing 1–2 at Tynecastle to a team called Birkirkara who came from Malta (yes, Malta!). They had seemed to have done the hard bit by earning a draw away from home the previous week, but tonight Tynecastle, not for the last time this season, resounded to boos from a support who, like them or loathe them, seldom seem to be given an easy ride by their players or their management. Little wonder that they are so bitter! And yet they have a loyal core of diehards who could walk away but, masochistically, they stay.

Meanwhile, across the North Sea in Brondby, Denmark, Hibs were going out on a penalty shoot-out. Hibs, eccentric as always, had parted company with their Manager Alan Stubbs in the immediate aftermath of him having broken the 114-year hoodoo and won the Scottish Cup for them! Even more eccentrically, in a less than totally smart career move, Stubbs went to Rotherham United for reasons that no one could explain, and was sacked after five months! There are things that simply do not lend themselves to rational explanation, but easier to understand was the fact that Stubbs' replacement Neil Lennon had to watch the second leg in the stand for bad behaviour in the first leg! Nothing changes there, then! But there was a genuine feeling of sympathy for Hibs, for they had lost the first leg at Easter Road, then brought it back in the second leg before going out in that most heart-breaking of ways (and one which is not unknown to Celtic fans) – a penalty shoot-out. Brondby incidentally contained one Teemu Pukki, a man familiar to Neil Lennon, for he had been at Celtic Park for a short, disappointing and underperforming time under Lennon's leadership.

Aberdeen did better, and their 1–0 win over Ventspils of Latvia guaranteed that Scotland would have two teams involved in Europe in August. Not exactly the stuff that makes one want to light bonfires of celebration in Stonehaven, Milltimber, Torry or Turiff, but at least something for them to look forward to!

Celtic now returned to Kazakhstan, this time to play Astana, having played Karagandy in 2013. It was a very long way away, not too far from China and Mongolia, but some Celtic supporters managed to get there, and they were rewarded with a draw, a result greeted with much joy among the support back home. The game had a tea-time kick-off and was available to be watched by the resourceful on a little-known satellite channel, and listened to on the radio by the less technically gifted. The pitch was artificial, something that perhaps causes more problems in the mind than anywhere else, and more potently, Celtic were up against a very strong team who scored first when Celtic fatally failed to defend a corner kick properly, raising – not for the first or last time – all sorts of arguments about that old chestnut 'zonal marking'.

Celtic now began to suffer a little, but crucially Astana failed to add to their lead. The radio commentator praised Craig Gordon time and time again for a series of saves, but all this proved for the support was the old adage that those of us of a nervous disposition find it a great deal more difficult to follow a game on the radio than on TV or in the flesh. It is never a good idea to listen to a game on a car radio when Celtic are playing, if you are driving! It is downright dangerous.

But then Celtic, with time running away, got a crucial away goal, brought about by the trickery and indeed the persistence of Patrick Roberts. The ball seemed to be going out of play on the by-line, but the defender, who could either have allowed the ball to go out or cleared it, did neither and Patrick Roberts nipped in and cut back to Leigh Griffiths, who teed the ball up to fire home with his left foot. Commentators tend to say 'priceless' before the words 'away goal'. That was exactly what this one was.

So Celtic flew home happy. They were involved at this time in a pointless (yet lucrative) pre-season tournament calling itself the International Champions Cup and involving games against Leicester City, Inter Milan and Barcelona. Celtic did badly in this competition, which has proved to be astonishingly easy to forget a year later, but there was a certain amount of TV coverage and therefore money, so it was hard to criticise the club for entering. The games were, however, little other than glorified friendlies. Everyone knew that the big show was the return leg when Astana came to Celtic Park on the night of Wednesday, 3 August.

A crowd of 52,000 was there, providing a fantastic atmosphere for what was a pulsating night's entertainment between two evenly matched sides, and Celtic scoring with two penalties at the end of each half. The one at the end of first half was scored by Leigh Griffiths after Kieran Tierney had been kicked at the edge of the penalty box. This gave Celtic a half-time lead, but then an odd (and very rare) error by the normally very reliable Craig Gordon allowed Astana to equalise on the night. He came out of his penalty box to head a ball clear. It hardly seemed necessary, but he made the fatal mistake of heading the ball down the centre of the park instead of to the side, and Ibraimi was able to lob the ball into the untenanted goal. It was a curious goal to lose, and it meant that the game was now heading for extra time and possibly penalties.

We were also uncomfortably aware that another goal for Astana would have meant curtains for Celtic's Champions League campaign, but Celtic, although not playing to their full potential as yet, were now the better and stronger side, and one would have fancied them to go through in extra time. In the event, it did not come to that, for Dembele was brought down in the box by a man with the unfortunate name of Shitov. It was his second bookable offence, so Dembele knew that even if he missed, Celtic would have a one-man advantage in the extra 30 minutes.

Why Griffiths was not given the penalty is not clear, but here we had the situation of the young Frenchman, just turned 20, with the awesome task of putting Celtic through. Deliberate time-wasting tactics were employed by the Kazak team with the intention of unsettling Moussa (another of them would eventually be sent off for arguing) but the young man showed no sign of nerves (even though all of us behind that goal did!) as he took a short run and put Celtic into the next round. It was the night that the 'Moussa Dembele' chant was born.

This could still have all gone horribly wrong, of course, for there was still another game to go before the sectional stages. But there was now a certain belief at Celtic Park that qualification could be achieved. Brendan had bought Kolo Toure in late July and he had made his debut that night in the second half against Astana. Possibly at the age of 35, the Ivorian was past his best, but Brendan had worked with him at Liverpool and knew that he would certainly be a positive influence in the dressing room. Kolo was a strict Muslim, but he was also a fun-loving but totally professional kind of a guy. He would seldom play this season, but his presence was priceless. The footage of him leading the Celtic players in the Yaya Toure/Kolo Toure song at the end of the season was a strong indication of just how large an influence he had.

Moussa Dembele.

The Scottish season was due to start the following weekend, and Celtic found themselves in the not entirely unfamiliar position of being the only Scottish team left in Europe. Aberdeen went out to Maribor on 4 August, the night after Celtic's triumph. One would have to agree that they did have a raw deal from the referee, but they also contributed to their own downfall by missing a penalty, conceding a grotesque goal at the end, and of course by their failure to finish off Maribor in the first leg at Pittodrie. It reminded one of the words of the old 1960s anti-war song, 'When will they ever learn?' It meant, however, that the Dons, still Celtic's main challengers in spite of the bogus revivalist moonshine that we heard from Ibrox, could now concentrate exclusively on the Scottish League.

But Celtic still had another hurdle to climb over before the sectional stage and that came in the shape of an Israeli team called Hapoel Beer-Sheva. There was an element of politics in this game as well. In recent years, Celtic fans, particularly the Green Brigade, had taken to flying the Palestinian flag. There had also been seen flying the flag of the Spanish Republic, which had fallen so grievously in 1939. Those who delight in this sort of thing would compare the Israeli occupation of

Palestine and the triumph of Nationalist Spain with the British occupation of Ireland – equally brutal and equally defended by those who managed to use the word 'civilisation' to excuse barbarism, and used religion as a tool of oppression as well – but the main reason why Celtic supporters flew the Palestinian flag was that the colour was predominantly green. More sinisterly, an Israeli flag had occasionally been seen at Ibrox! The media, sensing a story, tried to stir all this up, but minds were already concentrated on the game itself, the first leg to be played at Celtic Park on Wednesday, 17 August.

It was a tremendous display of attacking football, and Celtic won 5–2. By this time, Scott Sinclair had joined the club after a long and varied, but sadly unfulfilled, career with lots of English clubs (twelve of them, including loans), his problem having been that he had never been there for long enough with any team to settle down. Tonight, however, his influence was immediate and convincing. He was brought down when about to score and would surely have earned a penalty, but Tommy Rogic came up and scored in any case. Then Griffiths scored twice, once with a header and yet another direct from a free kick.

It was 3–0 at half-time and Celtic looked on easy street, as they left the field to one of the loudest rounds of applause at half-time that anyone had heard since the Jock Stein era. But then the old Celtic weakness of complacency in defence struck and the Israelis scored twice to make it a less happy 3–2. Celtic, however, stuck to their task, and late goals from Dembele and Brown made it 5–2. The Israelis, however, were no bad team and the away goals rule meant that 0–3 in Israel would put Celtic out of the European Champions League.

But oh, that second leg in Israel! Craig Gordon had already featured a great deal in Celtic's progress so far, and tonight, 23 August, was no exception. He saved an early penalty kick (the original offence was outside the penalty box but wrongly called a penalty by the Dutch referee), but then after Hapoel had scored a goal with a header, a horrible mix-up between Craig and right-back Saidy Janko allowed the Israelis to score again. This happened just at the start of the second half, and the rest of that 45 minutes was as tension-ridden an occasion as the team and the support had experienced for many years. Back home, with the game on live, TVs were shouted at (there was no answer to the very logical question of why one was shouting at an inanimate object!), carpets were worn away by constant tramping back and forward like a caged lion, cushions were gnawed and children were shouted at as the minutes ticked away with quite a few of us unable to bear the tension. The sight of the Celtic team in that awful black strip jumping all over each other at the end showed just how tense they had been as well.

The commentator, unschooled in political correctness, shouted tactlessly 'from one promised land to another', but this was how Celtic and their supporters all felt in Israel that night. At long last (it had, in fact, not been all that long – only two years) Celtic were back in the European elite, there would be loads of money and the club, the stadium and the support would now enjoy centre stage. Brendan Rodgers had only been with us for about three months, but he had already, at least, achieved something.

It had not really been a glorious campaign, but the vital aspect in it was the way in which it galvanised the support. Words like 'momentum' and 'morale' are only marginally less important than 'fitness', 'teamwork', et cetera, and given the close, intimate relationship between players and supporters at Celtic Park, the demeanour of the supporters is an indication of how the team are dong. The team had made a good start in Scotland as well, and in late August, Celtic supporters were happier than they had been for some time. One recalled an old pop song of the mid-1960s, with the lyrics 'something tells me I'm in for something good'. Herman's Hermits, if I remember correctly.

CHAPTER **FOUR**
A SOLID START

The Scottish League Championship was, of course, the bread and butter of the Scottish season. In recent years it had been called the Scottish Premier League, after the big boys had ill-advisedly broken away from the rest. But now everyone was back together again in one big, but not particularly happy, family, and what Celtic were going for seemed to be called the Premiership, whereas the second tier was now, confusingly, called the Championship. This was an idea imported slavishly from England. Beneath the 'Championship' were Divisions 1 and 2, and non-footballing people asked the fairly obvious question, 'Why can't they just be Divisions 1, 2, 3 and 4?' We had no answer to this question.

Not that it really mattered, for supporters talked about winning 'the League', and Celtic had done that for the past five years. Rangers had disappeared in 2012, but Celtic were already well ahead in the League that year anyway, and then for the next four years the main opposition had been Aberdeen, but in truth, apart from 2016, when Aberdeen put up a spirited but temporary resistance, the League had been won with little bother under Managers Neil Lennon in 2012, 2013 and 2014 and Ronnie Deila in 2015 and 2016.

Celtic had now won the League forty-seven times, still a few behind Rangers who had done well between the wars and in the early 1960s and early 1990s, when Celtic had themselves been crippled by incompetent management. The early years of this century had seen a dong-dong battle between the Glasgow sides, with neither able to stay on top for long. Those who argue against the Old Firm and talk rubbish about 'Glasgow conspiracies', et cetera, have little to be happy about when they look at the list of League winners, for beneath Celtic's forty-seven (in 2016) we drop to four League titles won by Hearts, Hibs and Aberdeen, and the most recent of them was 1985 when Alec Ferguson's Aberdeen won the title. Third Lanark, Motherwell, Kilmarnock, Dundee and Dundee United have all had one glorious triumph, and Dumbarton won it twice in the first two years (shared with Rangers in 1890) but the rest of Scottish League history is a gruesome catalogue of underachievement by the non-Old Firm teams.

As far as Celtic are concerned, the Scottish League is always looked upon as a possibility. Failure to win it is a disappointment, and indeed any long period of Rangers predominance is usually the result of something wrong at Celtic Park. Serious internal problems, for example, of complacency and lack of touch with reality were what allowed Rangers to win nine titles in a row from 1989–97, as Celtic, frankly, failed to match Rangers in anything. Further back, the 1950s and early 1960s showed a similar defeatist attitude on the part of Celtic management. Such things are hard for fans to forget, but by 2016, the boot was certainly on the other foot – even with the reappearance of the new Rangers.

The fixtures had been released in June, and it was noticed that Celtic's first game was against Hearts at Tynecastle. This was on the Sunday after Celtic had taken a big step forward on their journey for qualification to the sectional stage of the Champions League, so the support (or the small proportion of the support who were able to buy themselves a ticket) were buoyant as they made their way to Tynecastle, home of Scotland's chronic underachievers, Heart of Midlothian.

Hearts supporters are usually characterised by bitterness, particularly as far as Celtic are concerned. Several times I have met a Hearts supporter who was unaware of my affiliations, and would engage the gentleman or lady in general conversation about football. It would not be long before a disparaging, jealous and sometimes plain nasty remark was made about Celtic, whose position in the 'hate pecking order' is considerably higher than that of Hibs or anyone else. Rangers sometimes give the impression of being considered to be the natural allies of Hearts, whose less well-educated supporters throw around words like 'Fenian' or 'Catholic' without really having a clue what they mean! A former Hearts player, who had attended a Roman Catholic school in the west of Scotland, tells the story of how he was taking a corner kick at the Hearts end of the ground at Tynecastle. He raised one arm as the coded signal that this was to be a near post corner, and was amazed to hear 'Get your f***in' hand doon, ye Fenian b******!' – and this was from one of his own supporters!

In May 2011, late in the season, Celtic beat Hearts at Tynecastle. The game is remembered for the attack on Celtic Manager Neil Lennon by a 'headcase' from the front of the main stand. No one would blame Hearts or their management for this – because the man had problems, to put it mildly, and the incident was genuinely shocking – but a question really has to be asked about why some Hearts supporters cheered this event!

There are, of course, reasons for this irrational hatred of Celtic. There always was the Edinburgh–Glasgow component, and since the late 1960s, some Hearts supporters have started singing Rangers and Orange songs – something that is absolutely incongruous in Dalry and Gorgie, not to mention the Edinburgh middle class whom Hearts would normally aspire to woo. But there is bitterness as well, brought about by failure on the field. On at least three occasions, Hearts have 'blown up' on the last day of a season to throw away the League, and Celtic had a part to play in all three. Of course, 1986 was the day of Albert Kidd which we all know about, and 1959 had seen Hearts lose to a none-too-enthusiastic Celtic at Parkhead, thereby allowing Rangers, in an astonishingly ironic episode of history, to become champions!

But the worst 'throwing away of the League' came in 1965, when Kilmarnock came to Tynecastle needing to win 2–0, and did just that. Well done Killie, but what did it have to do with Celtic? Well, nothing really, except that it was the very day that Celtic won the Scottish Cup with Billy McNeill's header against Dunfermline, and on that day the hitherto underperforming Celtic and the always-potential-title-winners Hearts effectively changed places. Twenty months later, Celtic bought Willie Wallace from a spineless Hearts directorate, and the hatred of Heart supporters to Celtic was visceral and now more or less part of the lovely Heart of Midlothian stone near St Giles Cathedral! It is such a shame!

Historically, of course, Hearts could have been the 'establishment' team of Scotland. Twice League winners and four times Cup winners before 1907, and well ensconced in the capital, they could have been the 'Arsenal' of Scotland, supported by the wealthy and numerous Edinburgh bourgeoisie. As it was, they lost the Scottish Cup to Celtic in 1907 and then began an almost fifty-year trophy famine, which meant that the middle classes of the capital turned their love and affections to the Scotland rugby team. They were hardly likely to turn to Hibs! And Leith Athletic and St Bernard's were simply not good enough.

Famously, Hearts players enlisted almost en masse for the Great War. No one can doubt their bravery, although one has to qualify this, when one reckons that they would have been dragooned to the slaughter in any case a few years later. However, the gallantry of their men allowed their supporters to shout 'war dodgers' at Celtic teams, and there is the extraordinary myth that Hearts would have won the 1915 Scottish League if Celtic had had more men who 'joined up'. Frankly, this is unsustainable, for the Hearts players (most of them) had still not left Britain by April 1915, and were available for selection most Saturdays.

So there were and are reasons why Hearts hated Celtic. By the end of the first League game of the 2016/17 season they would have more cause, for Celtic triumphed 2–1. It was actually a fine game in the warm Edinburgh sunshine, with more than a little spice added by the fact that Scott Sinclair was making his domestic debut for Celtic, whereas Hearts introduced Tony Watt, scorer of a great goal for Celtic against Barcelona – but who had done little else for Celtic. He had returned from a disappointing sojourn in other lands, and he was now back in Scotland to play for Hearts.

It was James Forrest who opened the scoring for Celtic, although Hearts may have had a point when they claimed that there was a Celtic player (Stuart Armstrong) in an offside position and blocking their goalkeeper, but that was nothing compared with the controversy when Hearts were awarded a penalty after one of the most blatant dives that one is ever likely to see. Retrospective action was indeed taken against Jamie Walker, but he scored the penalty to level the score.

A total of eleven yellow cards were brandished – not all of them justified - by referee John Beaton, who was not having one of his better games – but with about

Scott Sinclair scores against Hearts at Tynecastle.

10 minutes remaining, Scott Sinclair turned in a cross from Leigh Griffths and immediately established a rapport with the Celtic fans by running towards them and doing high fives with them.

Hearts might have claimed a bit of hard luck in not getting a draw but any sympathy evaporated when the TV played back that horrendous dive. Tony Watt had missed a good chance with a header and had done little to persuade Celtic that they had made a mistake in letting him go. Celtic had looked good with their central-defenders of Eoghan O'Connell and Kolo Toure appearing quite solid, and Kieran Tierney continuing to impress. Callum McGregor looked good, as did Stuart Armstrong, something that was significant the longer the season went on, for neither had been too impressive last season under Ronnie Deila.

For those who bothered about that sort of thing, Celtic had had a good first weekend, for both Rangers and Aberdeen had drawn. Were we already on course for six in a row? Certainly, the season was well begun. The next League game was against St Johnstone, but it wasn't for another fortnight. Celtic had business on the European front, had to make a start to the Scottish League Cup, and more controversially didn't play a proper League game on Saturday, 13 August because they were still taking part in a tournament called the International Champions Trophy against Inter Milan.

This fixture, so reminiscent of 1967, was not nearly as prodigious as it seemed. It was played not at Celtic Park, nor the San Siro, nor even in Lisbon (where we would have loved it to be) but at Thomond Park, Limerick. A half-hearted, weakened Celtic side went down 0–2 to Inter Milan, and people were justified in wondering what on earth this was all about. It was on TV, and one had to give the commentators great credit for their Herculean efforts to try to convince viewers that this game was significant or important. Lisbon and 1967 were frequently invoked, but we were not to be fooled.

Partick Thistle were quite right to be angry. They were due to play Celtic that day, and resented the loss of prestige that they would have gained in being the first team to visit Celtic Park in a League fixture this season. (The game would eventually be played in midweek in December.) Apparently, every team was allowed to postpone one fixture in this respect – and to be fair, Aberdeen also took the opportunity to have a week off as well – but the other teams in the League felt, not without cause, that there was a little favouritism shown here to the bigger teams.

But the people who were really upset were the Celtic fans themselves, and they are a group of people whose feelings really should be taken into account. Here we had a lovely summer's day and everyone in Scotland playing football – but not Celtic! Celtic fans are prepared to swallow a certain amount of guff about 'pipe openers' and 'playing in a prestigious pre-season friendly' which means 'so much' to the club – in the month of July, when the season has not yet started. But this was August! It was time to get serious. As it was, Celtic's participation in this tournament may well have been lucrative, and it may have served a purpose in giving players a run, but as far as the fans were concerned, it was a total damp squib, and a waste of a Saturday. It also meant that, given Celtic's other commitments, it might not be too easy to rearrange a new date, particularly if the weather turned nasty in the winter. When this nonsense was not persevered with in 2017/18, there was a noticeable lack of protest or outcry!

And so it was off to the Fair City of Perth to play St Johnstone on Saturday, 20 August, for Celtic's second League game in the 2016/17 season. No one really can dislike St Johnstone. They are a club which punches far above its weight in the Scottish Premier League, in a city which, frankly, is not a footballing hotbed. It is a lovely city, but there is no great history of football success – until, that is, the 2013/14 season when they lifted the Scottish Cup for the first time in their history at Celtic Park (Hampden was being prepared for the 2014 Commonwealth Games) beating Dundee United. I think most Celtic supporters were glad to see that. Yes, yes, I know they wore blue...but then again, Dundee United wore orange! Anyway, the Saints triumphed.

Prior to that, all that St Johnstone had to show for themselves were two appearances some thirty years apart in League Cup Finals. They had played Celtic in October 1969 at Hampden, and fought well, but never recovered from an opening goal from Bertie Auld, and also found John Fallon in inspiring form in the Celtic goal. In 1999, they lost another League Cup Final to Rangers at Celtic Park.

Yet for Celtic in the great Stein years, it was openly said by several players at Celtic Park, notably the late Bobby Murdoch, that the Scottish team, other than Rangers, who gave Celtic the most bother was St Johnstone. They had quite a few wins over Celtic, particularly at their old ground of Muirton Park, which had the reputation of being the widest ground in Scotland and also one of the best playing surfaces. In April 1969, in a midweek fixture, the two sides played a marvellous game there with St Johnstone at one point, deservedly, being two goals up, but then Celtic pulled back to win 3–2. A year previously, similarly in a midweek fixture, Celtic had played marvellous football there to win 6–1.

Less happy memories for Celtic against St Johnstone came in 1936, when, in a result that astounded Scotland, St Johnstone put Celtic out of the Scottish Cup at Parkhead, and then twice St Johnstone inflicted damage on Celtic in the League Cup in season 1961/62, the game at Muirton triggering one of Celtic's most shameful nights of hooliganism as the frustrated fans went on the rampage. In autumn 1964, when Celtic were at a low ebb following a League Cup Final defeat by Rangers, Celtic conceded three soft goals in the first half to lose 0–3, and one can recall the looks of incredulity and amazement on the faces of St Johnstone fans. In 1981, St Johnstone also beat Celtic in the League Cup with a youngster called Ally McCoist giving the runaround to an unfortunate fellow called Willie Garner.

St Johnstone fans are not numerous. There is a distinct lack of nasty chants from them, and they have a large proportion of nice looking young women among them. Less happily, they are reputed to be the club in Scotland which has the highest proportion of people who vote Conservative. Perth is, of course, a rich city with a distinct lack of any kind of heavy industry, even from the days when everyone else in other parts of Scotland worked in factories, mines and shipyards. They like curling, horse racing and cricket as well. They are middle-class, bourgeois sort of people in the main.

In 1989, they gave up their home at Muirton Park (it is now a supermarket) and moved to McDiarmid Park on the west of the city, agreeably close to the motorway. One of their stands is called the Ormond Stand. This is as it should be, for Willie Ormond, that loveable wee man who played for Hibs in their great days of the 1950s, and later, of course, managed Scotland in the 1970s, was the man who pulled St Johnstone up from a struggling provincial outfit, frequently in the old Second Division, to being a respectable team which made a real impact on Scotland. And the Saints were not without their odd moment of glory in Europe.

And if St Johnstone had been blessed with a good Manager in the late 1960s, the same was true of 2016 when they were under the guidance of the big Ulsterman called Tommy Wright. Tommy had been with the Saints since 2011 and had been Manager since 2013, winning the Scottish Cup in 2014 and having had several other close calls with semi-finals, et cetera. He had also had a few health scares and was distinctly overweight. He had been a goalkeeper in his time as a player with many teams in England, and he also won thirty-one caps for Northern Ireland. In interviews, he always came across as a decent kind of a guy.

Celtic were aware that this St Johnstone team had, of course, beaten them towards the end of last season, with the League well won. Celtic might also have had their eye off the ball, given their European commitments, but they played a great first half in this lunchtime kick-off game. Some of us winced when we saw the awful black strips, but at half-time the team were 3–0 up and apparently on easy street with goals from Griffiths, Sinclair and a lovely run and finish from Forrest. The crowd was woefully small, and once again, we had to feel sorry for the St Johnstone management and players who surely deserved a bigger home support. It was also rather irksome for some Celtic fans, after the struggle that they'd had to find tickets, to then see the stadium half-empty. When St Johnstone were playing, say, Kilmarnock or Motherwell, it is quite embarrassing to see so many empty seats in what is still really a rather small, but compact, stadium.

Tommy Wright had clearly had a few things to say to his men, and they came out to put up more of a fight in the second half, but even so, Celtic seemed to be well in control, until well within the last 10 minutes they conceded a softish penalty. It was now 3–1, and that did not seem to be all that much of a problem, but then, in the 89th minute, St Johnstone got another – an undignified scramble to get the ball over the line with the Celtic defence not looking at all clever. Any chance, however, of a late equaliser for the Saints evaporated when substitute Ryan Christie, who had joined Celtic from Inverness, made it 4–2 in injury time.

It was, however, a good wake-up call for Celtic, who now had to realise that nothing could be taken for granted. Positives were the performances of Kieran Tierney and James Forrest and the now certain realisation that Scott Sinclair had been a good signing. The central defence, however, of Saidy Janko, Eoghan O'Connell and Kolo Toure would soon be replaced, for the second goal in particular looked bad. But as we left the Fair City that afternoon, we could reflect that the Scottish League this season had got off to a good start as we started to go for six in a row. But stern tests were appearing on the horizon in the shape of Aberdeen and Rangers, both about to pay their early-season visits to Celtic Park.

CHAPTER **FIVE**
TWO EARLY SUCCESSES

In the absence of Rangers following their administration/liquidation in 2012, Aberdeen had been Celtic's main challengers, as one would have expected. Historically, those who had hoped for a 'third force' to arrive in Scotland, had often looked east for the new challenge to come from Hearts or Hibs. Both of them had their moments of glory, but they were few and far between. North was the next direction to look, towards the Granite City. Occasionally a challenge had emerged from there, notably in the late 1970s and early 1980s when Alex Ferguson was their Manager and when Aberdeen was at the height of its economic powers. It had helped that Aberdeen was a very rich city, now basing its wealth on North Sea oil, rather than the traditional income sources of fishing and farming, although neither of these two industries had exactly gone away.

The 1980s had been a great era for the Dons and their successes had included a European one in 1983 when they won the Cup Winners' Cup (beating Real Madrid in the final!), and even after Ferguson was tempted away to Manchester United in 1986, the success did not entirely dry up for a few years with the Scottish Cup being won (in a painful penalty shoot-out against Celtic) in 1990, and the Scottish League Cup in 1989/90 and 1995/96. But the really good times had gone, the key moment being possibly the last day of the season at Ibrox in 1991, when the Dons might have won the Scottish League over Rangers. A draw might have sufficed, but they decided to blow up instead, intimidated by the Ibrox atmosphere and a subtle but effective campaign in the press. Aberdeen's League-winning triumph of 1985 remains the last time that any team outwith the Old Firm has been champions of Scotland.

The last few years of the century were bad ones for the Dons. They even managed to go out of the Scottish Cup to Stenhousemuir in 1995, flirted with relegation on several occasions, once being saved by League reconstruction (maybe they had 'knocked on a few doors' as well!) and in the year 2000, although they reached the finals of both Cup competitions, they were outclassed by Celtic in the League Cup and Rangers in the Scottish Cup. The League Cup Final of that year was likened to two old gentlemen who had fallen on bad times and fallen out with each other. They were then knocked over in the same road accident and now woke up to find their old enemy in the bed next to them! Celtic, still on their knees after the Inverness fiasco, were the least bad of the two of them and won 2–0.

Things went from bad to worse for them in the early years of the twenty-first century. There is a common perception in Scotland that Aberdonians are mean, moaning, greetin-faced pessimists. This is probably a false picture but nevertheless there was a certain validity of that picture in those awful years for the Dons where they were repeatedly let down by Managers. If anything (and this is an ambitious claim perhaps), they were even more guilty than Celtic of being taken to the cleaners by expensive foreign imports on whom not enough research had been done, and who were manifestly unsuited to the demands of the Scottish Premier League.

Their fans remained remarkably loyal. Their crowds were never great, and they were certainly capable of letting their players know all about it after a substandard performance, but they did stick with them. There were now and again a few members of the 'bawheid fringe' who called themselves silly things like 'casuals' and 'ultras', but their support was generally civilised.

Aberdeen's record against Celtic was particularly deplorable – at least their League record was, although on two occasions, in 2008 and 2014, they came to Parkhead and put us out of the Scottish Cup. Now and again they had a good result at Pittodrie against Celtic, but Parkhead was never a place where they gathered a lot of points in the Scottish League. In November 2010, they managed to lose 9–0 to a Celtic team which was good, but not great.

After a succession of, putting it as tactfully as possible, 'indifferent' Managers, the Dons appointed Derek McInnes in March 2013. He had recently been sacked by Bristol City but had been a reasonable success with St Johnstone in the past, and his first full season was a good one. Not only did he beat Celtic in the Scottish Cup in February 2014, but a month later he landed Aberdeen's only honour of the twenty-first century so far when he won the League Cup. It would be nice to say that it was a great triumph. In fact, it wasn't. It was a lacklustre final at Celtic Park which went to extra time and penalties, and Aberdeen were better at taking penalties than Inverness Caledonian Thistle (Celtic had unaccountably blown up against Morton earlier in the campaign).

McInnes and Aberdeen had also missed the boat, it was felt, in seasons 2014/15 and 2015/16. We have analysed in an earlier chapter these two seasons as far as Celtic are concerned. In both years, they won the League with a degree of comfort, but the way that they had played had not delighted their fans, especially in 2015/16, and particularly when Celtic hit a bad spell as January gave way to February in 2016. Celtic had (perhaps unluckily) gone out of the League Cup to Ross County in a Hampden semi-final and then on the following Wednesday night had lost a League match to Aberdeen at Pittodrie. The gap was now minimal and most pundits agreed that there was a 'title challenge'. The Dons fans that night had a banner saying, 'We're Coming To Get You!' Sadly for the red-and-white-clad, they didn't, and Celtic were allowed a few lifelines when Aberdeen let themselves down on a number of occasions, losing to teams like Inverness, Motherwell, Hearts and St Johnstone and generally letting Celtic and Ronnie Deila off the hook. As they had also gone out to Hearts soon after the New Year in the Scottish Cup, 2015/16 had been a bad season for the Dons.

Yet they had some fine players, especially the mercurial Johnny Hayes. Hayes, as it happened, was out injured when Aberdeen came to Parkhead on 27 August 2016, and he was sadly missed. The 57,578 crowd saw one big surprise to the Celtic line-up, for Craig Gordon was dropped and Dorus de Vries played in the goal instead. There had been several times in the season so far when Gordon had looked to be less in total command than we would have liked him to have been, and there certainly was an ongoing problem with his kicking and distribution, but he was still the best shot-stopper around, in the Scottish game at least, and the experiment of de Vries (who had of course played for Rodgers before at Swansea City) did not last long.

The weather was fine, the crowd was upbeat and enthusiastic for the team had qualified for the Champions League in midweek, and already praises were beginning to be sung about Brendan Rodgers. Celtic were in command for most of this game and thoroughly deserved their 4–1 victory. Leigh Griffiths opened the scoring, but then Adam Rooney pounced to level things after the Celtic defence had failed to clear a loose ball. It looked as if Aberdeen would go in at half-time on level terms, a scenario that would have flattered them, but then James Forrest, a man who had undergone a personality metamorphosis under Rodgers scored with a fine drive from the outside of his left foot.

Celtic remained on top for all of the second half, but we never felt totally secure until such time as Scott Sinclair scored a penalty after he himself had been brought down. Mark Reynolds of Aberdeen was sent off in the process, not that the tackle in itself was all that brutal, but more because he had already been booked for a rather nastier and more deliberate foul on Tom Rogic. Then, making 'assurance doubly sure', as they said in *Macbeth*, the same Tom Rogic, not for the first or last time in his life, broke Aberdeen hearts with a fourth from a free kick.

The importance of this game cannot be underestimated. Not only did it bring three points, but it set down a marker for the rest of the season. Aberdeen cannot but have been dispirited by this reverse, and everyone saw that Celtic were a force to be reckoned with, a great deal more enthusiastic and spirited than they had been last year, and the support a great deal more bubbly. A feature of the 2016/17 season would be the perpetual happiness of the support, in total contrast to last season. And of course, the next opponents after the International break (Scotland beat Malta 5–1) would be no less a team than the newly promoted Rangers!

St Valentine's Day 2012 had, of course, been the day that football in Glasgow changed. It was the day that Rangers went into administration, a necessary consequence of the corruption that encouraged dodgy dealing and the arrogance that made them think that somehow or another, they did not have to pay income tax! Then, in a move which defied all cynics who thought that everyone would be all old pals together and that no one would want to kill the goose that laid the golden egg, the other Premier League teams, spearheaded not by Celtic so much as by Dundee United, Motherwell and Hibs (each of whom had their own private issues and grudges against Rangers), forced relegation on them.

Thus 2012/13 was spent by Rangers in Division 2, 2013/14 in Division 1, 2014/15 and 2015/16 in the Championship (because they missed out in a play-off in 2015!), but now they were back. Technically, of course, they were not Rangers, and those who wanted them called Newco, Sevco or anything else were technically correct, but they still wore the same strip and they were, in fact, Rangers.

Since 2012, Celtic had played Rangers only twice, once in the semi-final of the League Cup of 2015 (won easily by Celtic) and once in the semi-final of the Scottish Cup in 2016 where Rangers triumphed after a penalty shoot-out after a distinctly un-Celtic-like performance from the men in green and white. It was this very game which triggered the departure of Ronnie Deila, although he was allowed to stay on and finish the job of winning the Scottish League.

It was an uncomfortable truth that Celtic in fact needed Rangers. Financial considerations apart, Celtic really need to be challenged, and challenged strongly, if they are to succeed in Europe. In 1967, what most people fail to realise (or choose to forget) is that Rangers, in fact, had a good team. Admittedly, they blew up badly at Berwick but they might well have won the League Cup in October 1966 and they took Celtic all the way in the Scottish League. And there was the undeniable fact that Rangers reached the final of the European Cup Winners' Cup. They lost, of course, but you do not get that far with a team of complete duffers!

When Rangers themselves won the Cup Winners' Cup in 1972, they were nowhere near any of the Scottish trophies (Celtic won a League and Cup double), and when Aberdeen did likewise in 1983, they were in fact third in the Scottish League! All this shows that if Scottish teams are to succeed in Europe, there must be a prerequisite of a strong challenge at home. Frankly, this had been lacking for Celtic for the last several seasons.

But apart from that, it was good to see Glasgow reinvigorated once more and the 'Old Firm' (even though some people hate that term and question its validity) game became almost the sole topic of conversation once again. It certainly got the juices and the hormones and everything else going once again. A game against Rangers was not just an ordinary fixture.

Traditionally, the first Rangers v. Celtic clash sets the tone for the season. One recalled with pride what history now calls the 'demolition derby' of 2000 when Celtic were three up in the first 20 minutes, and never looked back. It was the day of 'and the cry was no defenders' down Ibrox way, and Martin O'Neill's Celtic went on to lift a treble. On the other hand, one shudders to think of August 1988 and a 1–5 defeat. The defeat itself was bad enough, but the real damage lay in what happened next. Confidence was shattered and the old inferiority complex returned, plunging Celtic into years of misery – and this was after we had won a League and Cup double in spring 1988! A similar thing happened in August 1963 when, in the first game of the season, Celtic were on top until a defensive error allowed Rangers to score, Celtic then collapsed woefully and the season disintegrated even before it started.

Celtic were confident for this game on 10 September, and the bookies' favourites by some distance. Rangers, under Mark Warburton, a likeable Englishman far removed from the traditional hateful Rangers stereotype but simply not up to the job as events would prove, were a bunch of committed hard workers but lacking any big names and any obvious threat. They were still, in many cases, struggling to get over the psychological trauma of losing last season's Scottish Cup Final to Hibs in that game so much enjoyed by all of us, when Celtic men Anthony Stokes and Liam Henderson (not to mention Manager Alan Stubbs) played such a part in the demise of Rangers. Rangers were back in the Premier League, but had failed so far to set the heather on fire. Celtic, on the other hand, had looked very impressive against Aberdeen.

But Rangers had brought in a character called Joey Barton. To say that Barton was a controversial character is an understatement. He had the capacity to attract trouble in a way reminiscent of the way in which dog turds attract bluebottle flies. Gambling, racism, homophobia, prison, sexism and violence are all there for anyone who cares to browse his Wikipedia entry, but he was a reasonable player, although now one had to feel that his best years were behind him. He immediately became a cult figure with the Rangers support, and much was made of the coming game and his inevitable confrontation with Scott Brown. It hardly needs telling who won that particular duel!

If the game in 2000 was the 'demolition derby', this game was the 'demolition derby mark 2', or as some would call it, the 'Dembelition derby', after the part played in it by Moussa Dembele, a young man who won his spurs here (if he had

Moussa Dembele.

not done so before) and earned a place in Parkhead immortality by scoring a hat-trick against Rangers. This put him immediately in the same bracket as Harry Hood, Stevie Chalmers, Billy McPhail, Malky MacDonald and Jimmy Quinn – and that was not bad company!

It is a moot point whether Moussa would have been playing that day if Griffiths had not been injured, but he certainly took his opportunity on the bright sunny day at Celtic Park with a midday kick-off. The fact that the game was on TV meant that the rest of Scotland, England and indeed the world had the opportunity to see the game before moving on to see their own games. They would have been mightily impressed.

Dembele scored the first goal on the half-hour mark with a powerful header from a corner. The commentators and scribes lamented Rangers inability to defend set pieces, corner kicks in particular, but this does less than credit to the accurate Sinclair corner kick and Dembele's acute positional sense and indeed his strong McGrory-type header. But it was his second goal just before half-time which made everyone sit up and take notice. Nir Bitton picked up a loose ball and released Dembele who beat Senderos, then seemed to throw it all away as he manoeuvred for a better position before crashing home to release delirium in the stands.

But then, on the very stroke of half-time, Rangers pulled one back through a combination of Kenny Miller and a guy wearing (ludicrously) a black headband. Their noisy supporters felt that this gave them a chance, but it was Celtic who struck in the second half as Scott Sinclair picked up a good Dembele pass. Phillipe Senderos of Rangers then got sent off for an incredibly stupid handball, their Assistant Manager Davie Weir was invited to watch the rest of the game from the stand, and then with Celtic now well on top, Moussa Dembele got his hat-trick from a Lustig cross. He was booked for over-celebration by the ever-officious referee Willie Collum, but then the very impressive Stuart Armstrong made it five just at the end of the game after a good pass from Kieran Tierney.

This was a great day for Celtic under the Parkhead sun. The defeat of Aberdeen a couple of weeks ago could have been fairly said to have 'crippled' Aberdeen's challenge for the Premiership. Today without a shadow of a doubt killed the pretentions of Rangers. They were defeated in such a way that they were not likely to recover, outclassed by Celtic in every single area of the field. More important than the three points gained was the propaganda effect. From now on, newspapers and radio and TV pundits began every article or programme with the premise that Celtic would win the League.

Rangers, of course, had every reason to believe that, but for Celtic it was not necessarily a comfortable position. Celtic always have to guard against complacency, and our history is absolutely littered with examples of Celtic teams who have come to grief by taking the opposition too lightly. One thinks of many Scottish League Cup Finals thrown away and Scottish Cup exits to inferior opposition, and Brendan Rodgers now had the massive task of keeping everyone's feet firmly on the ground. This, of course, included supporters.

Yet there was so much to be happy about. Sinclair and Dembele had fitted in seamlessly and the results had been spectacular. Several players, notably Stuart Armstrong and James Forrest who had struggled to produce consistent form under Ronnie Deila, were now far more impressive. Kieran Tierney was a class act, and although the central defence had yet to settle down, there was a new solidity in the defence. Nir Bitton, Callum McGregor, Tommy Rogic and Liam Henderson were possibly not necessarily automatic selections, but were good enough. And, of course, leading them all was Scott Brown, an inspiring captain who had now, seemingly, also acquired the art of self-restraint. Hardly anyone noticed that Stefan Johansen had departed to Fulham in late August. He had been with us for two and a half years. Deservedly the winner of many awards in the 2014/15 season, 2015/16 had been a disappointment with injury and loss of form.

The domestic season had been well begun. But now it was necessary to turn our attention to Europe. That would be different altogether!

CHAPTER **SIX**
THE EUROPEAN ADVENTURE

A couple of days after Celtic's qualification for the sectional stages, the draw was held. The co-efficient was still making its baleful presence felt, however, and Celtic were in the fourth pot in the rigged draw. Even at that, we felt that we were unlucky to find ourselves against Manchester City, Barcelona and Borussia Monchengladbach. A tad more difficult than Inverness Caledonian Thistle, Dundee and Hamilton, one would have to say!

First up were Barcelona in the Nou Camp. Maybe it was as well to get the difficult one out of the way first, we thought, and those who travelled to the capital of Catalonia for the game on 13 September were on a high, having just seen the 'dembelition derby' on 10 September in which Celtic had delivered a 5–1 thrashing to Rangers. The season had, undeniably, been well begun, but how would the new Celtic do against a team that would have to be described as 'top class' in any world context?

Hannibal of Carthage was the man who crossed the Alps with elephants, as we all learned at school, but perhaps his most lasting contribution to the world was the building of the city on the banks of the Ebro. Hannibal's family name was Barca, hence the name of the new city called Barcelona. The city had a long and remarkable history. In the twentieth century, it had experienced a genuine social revolution in 1936 in the Spanish Civil War, when it declared strongly for the Republic. Food and clothing were distributed free, women were given equal rights, and the word 'adios' for 'cheerio' was frowned upon, because 'dios' was the word for God, and the Roman Catholic Church was not held in any high esteem! Sadly, the revolution did not last long, for the anarchists, communists and Catalan nationalists all fell out with each other, and the city succumbed to the Nationalist army of General Franco in early 1939. Thus began unimaginable horrors of persecution and repression.

But one of the things that made the repression bearable for the Catalans was football, and their team slowly rose again to challenge the Real Madrid so beloved of General Franco. Today 'el clasico' is the name given to the Spanish 'old firm' encounter, and it seldom disappoints. Perhaps surprisingly, Barcelona have only won the European Cup five times, lagging a long way behind Real Madrid, and their first triumph was as late as 1992, some twenty-five years after Celtic! In the twenty-first century, however, they have been triumphant on four occasions, on three of these occasions beating English sides (Manchester United twice and Arsenal once) in the final.

Celtic have always got on well with Barcelona. There is a footballing connection in Henrik Larsson, but they also in the past, at least, have shared a certain 'anti-establishment' feeling. It is often said that Celtic supporters (with justification in some cases, but not always) have a chip on their shoulder about Rangers and the SFA. These feelings are replicated in Catalonia as far as Real Madrid and the Spanish football authorities are concerned.

But no one could deny that Barcelona were a class act with men like Neymar, Iniesta, Suarez (familiar, of course, to Brendan Rodgers, and now reinstated after his 'biting' performance of a few years ago) and Lionel Messi whom many said was the best in the world. But then again, they maybe hadn't seen Jimmy Johnstone or Bobby Murdoch! Tonight's game was an embarrassment, as Celtic went down 0–7. As often happens, a lifeline of sorts was offered which might have at least limited the damage in the shape of a penalty kick, but Moussa Dembele, the hero of a few days ago, brought himself down to earth by missing it. Those who had travelled to see this game could console themselves with Catalan hospitality, while those of us who had stayed at home were watching some drama on BBC long before the final whistle.

It was Celtic's heaviest European defeat, and on a par with the infamous 0–8 to Motherwell in 1937 and 1–8 to Rangers in 1943. The 1–8 defeat was in wartime when far more important things were going on in Africa and Stalingrad, and the 0–8 was on a Friday night before the players (who had won the Scottish Cup the week before) were about to board an overnight train to go to watch the English Cup Final between Sunderland and Preston, and it was widely believed that celebrations of their own Scottish Cup triumph had left their mark!

There was, however, no excuse for this one, which raised serious questions about Scottish football and questioned Celtic's very credibility as a European power. Yet, even in the middle of all this humiliation, there was some kind of opportunity for Brendan Rodgers to examine his team. Questions now began to be asked about Dorus De Vries, and Kolo Toure was now generally agreed to be past his best. But the biggest problems that had to be faced were the psychological problem of believing in themselves again and the need to realise that, as we were now at the top European table, thorough professionalism was required with the absolute necessity of making no mistakes. The ball, for example, must never be given away, and opponents must always be marked!

The psychological problem was a very real one. It was very easy, if one watched insidious English-based programmes, to believe that Scottish football was some kind of irrelevance, and that Celtic, who had been, of course, very lucky to qualify from this so-called inferior League, were really only there on sufferance, and that it was a matter of time before they were knocked out. Famously, fifty years earlier, Jock Stein had knocked that nonsense on the head. It was now the task of Brendan Rodgers to do the same.

Funnily enough, that 0–7 hammering did not necessarily affect Celtic too adversely, or at least it didn't need to. Two clubs qualified, and Celtic's next opponents on 28 September would be Manchester City. The first time these clubs met, the game would be played at Celtic Park and we braced ourselves for all the clichés that come our way when a Scottish team plays an English team, the most likely being stuff about 'the auld enemy' and 'the Battle of Britain'!

Manchester City were another team which had, like Liverpool, suffered when Alex Ferguson was the Manager of Manchester United. Too often they had been the rabbit paralysed in the car's headlights, and they had caused their fans untold distress. Indeed, as far as trophy winning was concerned they had been virtually eclipsed. Between 1976 and 2011, they had won absolutely nothing, and that was in spite of throwing money at everything in a desperate effort to break their appalling self-inflicted cycle of underachievement. Since winning the English Cup in 2011, they had redeemed themselves to a certain extent and had been the champions of England in 2012 and 2014, their 2012 triumph coming on that never-to-be-forgotten day when Sergio Aguero scored with the last kick of the Premiership season to pip Manchester United, and to get that particular monkey off their back at long last. That particular Sunday was tremendous television.

Celtic could at several points in their history identify with City's problems. There were a few other connections. Billy McNeill had been at City for an unsuccessful spell in his interregnum between 1983 and 1987 (but then again, Billy was too much of a Celt to be successful anywhere else!) and in 1904, Celtic had won the Scottish Cup and Manchester City the English Cup a week later. Celtic had been managed by Willie Maley and Manchester City by his elder brother Tom Maley, who had of course himself played for Celtic. It appears to have been unique for brothers to manage the Scottish Cup and the English Cup winners in the same season.

In 2016, Pep Guardiola was the Manager of Manchester City and they were doing well at the top of the English Premiership when they came to Celtic Park on 28 September. In fact, 'doing well' was an understatement. Their record was 100 per cent and that included their defeat of Borussia Monchengladbach a fortnight previously. They were impressive, and Pep Guardiola was one of those Managers with a tremendous European pedigree whom one did not very readily associate with the concept of 'defeat'.

The game on a fine autumn night at a packed, noisy and upbeat Parkhead before 57,592 fans (and the game could have been sold twice over if there had been a stadium big enough) was a tremendous advert for both teams and was thoroughly enjoyed by football fans on their TV screens all over Europe and beyond. The final score was 3–3, but the game could well have gone Celtic's way at several key points, and the know-all English pundits departed without sneers at Scottish football and with a new found respect for Celtic who, they grudgingly admitted, would be able to hold their own in the English Premiership. It would have been nice to win, but Celtic supporters got into their cars and buses that night satisfied with a good night's work.

Apart from anything else, Celtic had been true to themselves and to our tradition of attacking football. There had been none of the timidity and self-doubt so sadly visible at the Nou Camp. They had 'gone at' City, and had three times been ahead, sadly being pegged back on all three occasions. Moussa Dembele was tremendous, for it was he who scored the first and the third goals, both coming at the start of each half. To be fair, the first goal really should have belonged to Erik Sviatchenko, whose powerful header was probably going wide before it hit Dembele on the chest and went in, but the third goal was a tremendous piece of classy football, as Dembele, with his back to the goal, brought the ball down and hooked it homewards. In between that Kieran Tierney, whose development at this level was nothing short of the speed of an express train, charged down the left wing and hit a ball which took a wicked deflection off Raheem Sterling and went in.

Against that, Manchester City's first goal may have had a touch of offside about it, but the second goal was sheer class from Raheem Sterling just a few minutes after he had conceded his own goal. A moment's slackness in the Celtic defence conceded the third goal, but it was difficult to criticise the Celtic defensive pairing of Kolo Toure and Erik Sviatchenko who had been brilliant throughout. Another man who played brilliantly, in his case because he had a point to prove, was Craig Gordon, who had now been reinstated in the Celtic goal.

This was breath taking stuff and it was a game that will live long in the memory of all who saw it. It was the game in which Celtic regained their self-respect following the Barcelona disaster, and the fact that Barcelona had defeated Borussia Monchengladbach in Germany that night meant that Celtic were a point ahead of the Germans when they were due to come to Celtic Park in three weeks' time. It was generally agreed that Barcelona would win the section, but there was now nothing certain about Manchester City joining them. A great deal of football remained to be played in this section, now generally agreed throughout Europe to be the most difficult and the most exciting of them all.

Celtic and their fans had come out of this game well. The noise was tremendous throughout the 90 minutes and the stadium looked good on TV, as it always did on a European night. The crowds and traffic jams around the ground were horrendous, but that was the price of success, and we could reflect on just how far we had come this season so far. And there was a long way to go yet.

All this optimism was quickly dispersed on 19 October, when Borussia Monchengladbach came to Glasgow for the third game in the Champions League. Celtic had no great connections with this German side, and many were the jokes about no one being able to spell their name and how the most unpopular man at their home games was the man who shouted out 'Give us a B...give us an o...give us an r...' – and how many letters would there be on a scoreboard if they ever played Alania Vladikavkaze?

This was a crucial stage in Celtic's season. League form was consistently good with only one point lost, but a complicating factor may have been the imminent semi-final in the Scottish League Cup against Rangers at Hampden. It was due to take place on the Sunday after the game against Borussia Monchengladbach, and however much everyone insisted that it was 'one game at a time', nevertheless a Rangers game is massively important, and perhaps more so than even a Champions League game. It did prey upon minds.

The Borussia Monchengladbach game was a massive disappointment for the 57, 814 who turned up and a puzzlement for the millions who watched it on TV. Celtic's big mistake was to give the Germans too much respect when, as later events would prove, they were not all that great a team and might well have cracked under the sort of pressure that Celtic applied against Manchester City, for example. Instead, we had a Celtic side who curiously failed to rise to the eager expectations and support of the fans, and whose midfield failed to grasp and retain the initiative. It was a curiously uncharacteristic Celtic performance, and by the end of the first half the crowd at Parkhead had gone ominously silent.

Nevertheless, in spite of all that, the situation at half-time was not disastrous. Indeed, it had been Celtic who had had the best chance when Scott Sinclair blasted over the bar after a good move, and in any case, we consoled ourselves with the reflection that European games frequently were a game of cat and mouse in the early stages. The main action was yet to come.

The second half started with the Green Brigade, as always, behind the team and for a spell there was a slight improvement, although there was still no control of the game. But then came a couple of disasters, and how it hurts to point the finger of blame at Kolo Toure, the gentle Ivorian who had done so well for the club up to now. A ball seemed to be going out of play on the goal line. Kolo might have conceded a corner, allowed the ball to go out or turned round and belted it up the park. In the event he did none of these, and a Borussia attacker nipped in to rob him of the ball and slip it across to a teammate to score. It was the sort of thing that Toure would have got off with in a more mundane, domestic Scottish League game – but this was the Champions League!

Even after this the cause was not yet lost and now, in quick succession, Rodgers brought on Callum McGregor, a slightly more attack-minded player than Nir Bitton, then Leigh Griffiths and Paddy Roberts for James Forrest and Tommy Rogic, as Celtic endeavoured to move forward for an equaliser that would mean so much to them. But the 77th minute killed it all, when poor Kolo Toure made another howler with an attempted clearance, rightly described as 'sloppy' by Chris Sutton (his favourite word, one felt!) and the Germans scored again.

There was now no way back, and the crowd began to move disconsolately to the exits as the minutes ticked away. Full time brought misery to the crowd, so reminiscent of other heart breaking European nights in the distant and not so distant past. Kolo Toure was obviously singled out as being too 'old' or too 'casual' and certainly too 'sloppy', but it was less than fair to Kolo to blame everything on him. The blame had to be shared and it was one of these nights when, quite simply, too many players had an off night. To his credit, Brendan Rodgers faced the media, admitted it was a bad night and refused to take the easy option of blaming everything on Kolo Toure, whom he praised for his past record.

So where did this leave Celtic at the halfway stage, with two home games played? Frankly, it was difficult to see how they were going to qualify for the Champions League last sixteen, and even the Europa League was now a big ask. Celtic always played better at home than away, and they had yet to travel to Germany and Manchester. And yet there was the feeling that Celtic could play a lot better than their results would suggest. Certainly, the Manchester City game gave them a great deal of hope, and although any chances of a good result against Barcelona were slim (and yet they had done it before as recently as 2012), it was now incumbent upon them to go to Borussia and show Europe that they were not as bad as they seemed. The problem against Borussia at Parkhead had been one of attitude – not in any discipline sense or lack of effort, but more in lack of conviction that they could do it.

It is, of course, very important to have 'a guid conceit o themselves' as they say in Scotland. This had been lacking that night. One must never go into a game thinking that one is going to lose. That is emphatically not the Celtic way, and the whole experience was a profoundly chastening and depressing one, but one from which the team had to take a lesson, and the support had to recover from. Because of the way that fixtures were arranged, the next game was against Borussia in Germany. A win there would put us back in contention for a Europa League place, certainly, and that would be something, but in the meantime, in the more immediate future, there was a Scottish League Cup Final semi-final at Hampden, followed hard on its heels by a trip to Ross County (not as easy a game as it sounded) and then a fixture that no one thought would be easy or straightforward – a trip to Pittodrie to play Aberdeen.

These potential problems had been dealt with and overcome by the time that Celtic travelled to Germany on 1 November. They had never won on German soil, but this night was as close as it was ever likely to happen for them, for it was a fine battling performance against a stronger German side than had faced them two weeks ago when they had several men out through injury. The way that Celtic played that night to earn a well-merited draw made it all the more galling that they had played so timidly against them at Parkhead two weeks ago. Ironically, too, it was the night on which they played arguably their best football in Europe this season, but it was also the night when it became apparent that only a miracle would allow them to play in Europe under any circumstances in the New Year.

Celtic had started well, with Scott Sinclair distinctly unlucky to hit the woodwork, but then failure to mark adequately saw them go behind. Most of us watching on TV (and the large Celtic support which had travelled to Germany) were reconciled to a beating but it speaks volumes for the team that they did not buckle. They fought back. They were unlucky on several occasions before Dembele was held back by an opponent in the box. It was perhaps not really deserving of a red card, but a penalty it certainly was. Dembele himself took it and scored. Celtic were now in the ascendancy, and things would have been so much different if the fast-improving Callum McGregor, who had come along by leaps and bounds this autumn, had not pulled his shot wide late in the game. It would have put them two points ahead of Borussia and given them a realistic chance of qualification for the Europa League, although it was now clear that Manchester City would join Barcelona in the Champions League.

As it was, Celtic still had a slight chance of making it to the Europa League, although the odds were decidedly against them. Perhaps it was true that Celtic were not as yet quite ready for a European campaign after the New Year – the Europa League in particular would have seen a heavy commitment of fixtures – but there was a certain feeling growing among the support and in Scottish football in general that the day was not now far away in a season or two when Celtic would be once more jousting with giants in a European context.

It was difficult playing in Europe, and yet simple at the same time. The elimination of mistakes was the obvious area on which one had to work. Another was the ability to play possession football and to spend time simply passing the ball to each other. Chances also had to be taken. All these things were far more important than the concept of having a 'good team'. The super mega-bucks teams could actually be counteracted and even defeated on the field by a hard-working outfit who knew and practised the basics. There also had to be belief! Mental strength was an important thing.

In the event, however, it was Barcelona who delivered the coup de grace at Celtic Park on 23 November. The 2–0 defeat to the Catalan giants meant that although Celtic could equal the points tally of Borussia Monchengladbach, the Germans would win on the 'direct matches' rule, something that brought us back once again to that very unfortunate and lacklustre game of 19 October at Celtic Park. Tonight, the most impressive thing was probably the atmosphere at the beginning, although one would have to admit that the plucky Celtic team never gave up, and defeat, when it came, was accepted with dignity and respect. We left Europe 'with our heads held high' in the words of the awful cliché of the day.

There was a clear determination that there would be no repeat of the embarrassment suffered at the Nou Camp. There was determination and commitment, with Scott Brown in particular quite prepared to land a few hefty tackles on Barcelona players rather than allowing them to come at Celtic, which had led to our downfall in September. But it was Barcelona who went ahead with what has to be admitted was a good ball from Neymar to Messi, who seemed to have found about an inch of space to do the needful. Craig Gordon then had a remarkable one-handed save from Luis Suarez before half-time.

If you are to do anything against Barcelona, you must take every opportunity that is given to you. It will be recalled that Dembele missed a penalty against the Catalans in the Nou Camp, and tonight the same player missed the opportunity for Celtic to equalise when a fine cross from James Forrest found his head, but Dembele did not get enough power on it, and the young Frenchman headed weakly into the hands of the goalkeeper. Nevertheless, it showed that Celtic were fighting.

The game finished, however, when Emilio Izaguirre (Kieran Tierney was out injured) brought down Suarez in the box. Suarez was exactly the man to make the most of all this, and Messi converted the penalty kick. The game now petered out. Possibly Barcelona might have scored again, but a big talking point was why

Neymar, already on a yellow card for a clash with Lustig, did the same again and was not given the invitation to depart the scene.

The Celtic fans stuck with the team to the end, but the game did not end on the happy, loving note that previous Celtic v. Barca games had ended on. Indeed, the Celtic fans turned on Neymar (there had been a little 'previous' with him, of course, involving Scott Brown) and other perceived cheats like Suarez with various jokes being made about him not lacking any 'bite'. All this, of course, did not hide the rather unpalatable fact that Celtic were now out of Europe. It had not been a total disaster, and one hoped that lessons had been learned, but it was a disappointment nevertheless. It had now to be totally pushed to one side and relegated to the back of one's mind, for the Scottish League Cup Final was now approaching on Sunday.

There followed one not entirely unpleasant little postscript to Celtic's European campaign, and that was a trip to Manchester City's Etihad Stadium for what was now little more than a friendly, for Manchester City were now in the Champions League and the game meant little for them. On the other hand, it was Scotland v. England, and Celtic mobilised a huge support (far more than the tickets available) for the trip to Lancashire on Tuesday, 6 December.

It was actually a good game, finishing 1–1 after two early goals, one a brilliant individual run from Patrick Roberts to make a point to his parent club perhaps, and then a few minutes later, Iheanacho scored an equally good goal. After that, play was even and there were chances at both ends. Manchester City scored but were flagged offside, Celtic were denied a clear penalty when Roberts was held back by Clichy, and a couple of half chances fell the way of Leigh Griffiths and Gary Mackay-Steven, but it was not to be. The important thing, however, was that Celtic had won back their self-respect in Europe.

What made that night for Celtic was the fans. The ticketless ones more or less took over all of central Manchester to watch the game in pubs, and those who were at the ground had infiltrated the City sections of the ground to a very large extent, as became apparent when the mobile phones were held up with their light on at the 67th minute. It was a very moving experience, and some Manchester City supporters had clearly never seen anything like that before.

The unacceptable side was the behaviour of some of our guys who indulged in 'scuffles' with the locals, as it was tactfully put. There were three mitigating factors – one was that it was very definitely a minority, the other was that the Manchester City fans also had a minority who were just as bad (the English educational system not seeming to be any great success either!), and the third was a certain amount of provocation by the Manchester authorities who did things, for example, like keeping Celtic fans penned in for an unconscionable time after the game was over. Manchester police, of course, had long memories from 2008, when the UEFA Cup Final was played at that very ground between Rangers and Zenit Saint Petersburg. Serious damage and rioting had happened that night, and very sadly, all Glasgow fans were tarred with the same brush in the eyes of the Constabulary.

But as we headed home in the early hours of the morning, we reckoned that several lessons were to be learned about Europe, and they were all simple ones. Don't make mistakes, don't overestimate your opponents (for any team on earth can be beaten), don't go into a game defeated before you start, and take advantage of every chance that comes your way. Simple, isn't it?

Celtic had won three points. In four of the six games (excluding the Barcelona games, perhaps), things could have been a great deal better if Celtic had been a little more 'savvy' of the ways of the European world. They could also have done with a little more of that indefinable but ever-present quality called 'luck'. Yes, I know to a certain extent you make your own luck, but sometimes the world is simply against you, and you have to deal with it until such time as the tide changes.

But enough of such philosophy. Europe is over, but Scotland had still a great deal to offer. Time to sleep, for the drunken guy on the bus has fallen asleep in mid-chorus of 'Sean South of Garryowen', and everything is all quiet apart from the hum of the minibus heading north on the M6. We have our self-respect. Partick Thistle on Friday night is the next game.

CHAPTER **SEVEN**
THE LEAVES TURN YELLOW BUT EVERYHING ELSE IS GREEN

Celtic's first game after their return from the Barcelona debacle was at Inverness. It is always very pleasant (apart from in the depths of winter) to travel up the A9, passing scenery so far removed from industrial Central Scotland as to appear almost a different world. Inverness is a fine city, but until comparatively recently not a hotbed of Scottish football. Yet there had been Peter McWilliam, a name not immediately obvious to the current generation but a great player for Newcastle United and Scotland before the First World War, and totally deserving of the nickname of 'Peter the Great'. Apart from that great man, very little, and it had only been as late as 1994 that the two Inverness teams, Thistle and Caledonian, had agreed to merge and form a club that would, undeniably, make its mark on the Scottish game.

On at least four occasions since 1994, they had caused Celtic serious distress. There had, of course, been the infamous night of 8 February 2000 which had, in retrospect, had to happen so that John Barnes could be replaced by Martin O'Neill, but then Martin O'Neill himself made a horrendous misjudgement in his team selection for a Cup tie in March 2003. Flushed with success against Liverpool in the UEFA Cup, Celtic had gone to Inverness and exited the Scottish Cup, having seriously underestimated the power of Inverness Caledonian Thistle. It was a curious team selection, and has to go down as one of Martin's (rare) bloomers, and effectively handed Rangers the treble in that year. More recently, the League in 2011 would have been won but for a strange and irrational Celtic performance in Inverness late in the season, and then, of course, we all had vivid memories of the goal that we should have had, and the sending off of Craig Gordon in the Scottish Cup semi-final of 2015. Not all our memories of Inverness were happy ones, but we had also played some good games in the Highland capital as well.

At one point, Inverness Caledonian Thistle, when they first joined the Scottish Premier League, had to play all their home games at Pittodrie, a distance of over

100 miles away. This was incredible but true, and said a great deal about the mentality of those who ran Scottish football in those days, but now Inverness were well established – up to a point. Their ground, with a dual carriageway on one side and the sea on the other, was an unusual one to say the least. The Celtic end would be packed, there would be loads of elbow room at the Inverness end and in the Main Stand. Across from the Main Stand, there would be not very much apart from a television gantry, a cabin or two, a toilet or two and limited accommodation for about 100 spectators in what they called the West Stand, which was exposed to the elements! Yet there was some character to the ground as well, and it was totally different from any other ground we had ever been at.

We'd had a bad few days of it from workmates about losing 7–0 to Barcelona, but there was no reason to expect an adverse reaction when we arrived in Inverness on Sunday, 18 September. Time was when the Free Church and others might have organised protests about this profanation of what they called the Sabbath, but these days had now long gone. The crowd was small – 6,061 – and we wondered how on earth Inverness Caledonian Thistle survived. The weather was bleak but still fairly mild, and the pitch looked in good condition.

The game started quietly enough, but Celtic gradually assumed control, and in 17 minutes, Kieran Tierney crossed for Tom Rogic to put Celtic ahead. This looked comfortable enough, but Billy King equalised from outside the box on the left to level things, and then Inverness felt ill done by when Ross Draper went down on the edge of the box. TV replays showed that there had been some contact made by Erik Sviatchenko but possibly not enough to warrant a penalty kick and/or a red card, and one felt that referee Don Robertson had got that one right. Then, before half-time, we had a superb goal from Scott Sinclair who picked up a ball in his own half, then ran all the way with the ball to the edge of the penalty box to curl home an unstoppable shot.

This was superb stuff, and when Celtic went in at half-time, it was difficult to see any result other than a decisive victory for the green and white. Indeed, but for Fon Williams in the Inverness goal and the woodwork on at least two occasions, Celtic would have increased their lead as they totally dominated the game. But, as is frequently the case – and how often have we seen it? – if you don't take advantage of your territorial possession and dominance, the other team can nip up and score. This is precisely what happened here as time was running out. An Inverness corner was not properly cleared by the Celtic defence and the ball came back to Greg Tansey, who sent over a ball for Alex Fisher to score the equaliser.

It was a disappointment. The defence had been caught out, but this was Jozo Simunovich's first game back after a prolonged injury lay-off and perhaps he and rest of the defence were not quite sharp enough. In any case, more and more questions were asked about Dorus de Vries in the goal, who seemed to lack the command that Gordon had. The disappointment was all the more acute in view of the amount of play and possession that Celtic had enjoyed throughout the game, but it was the first two points dropped in the Scottish League this season, and we would find that it would be a long time before we experienced another disappointment.

It had been a funny kind of a week for Celtic. Eight days ago, they had defeated Rangers 5–1, then had experienced a totally different kind of emotion as they went down 0–7 to Barcelona, and now here was a draw against our old foes from the north. Not that it really seemed to matter, however, for Celtic were now three points ahead of second-place Hearts – and had a game in hand! There was a League Cup encounter with Alloa in midweek, and then Kilmarnock were due to appear at Celtic Park next Saturday.

No one could say that Kilmarnock had a good record at Celtic Park. They had gone from 10 December 1955 until 27 October 2012 – almost 57 years – without winning at Celtic Park. They'd had a few draws in that time at Celtic Park, had won the League Championship in 1965, the Scottish Cup in 1997 and the League Cup in March 2012, but victories at Celtic were as rare as hen's teeth for the Kilmarnock men. Rugby Park, on the other hand, had always been a tough place for Celtic to visit. Indeed, it was the scene of a 0–6 thumping in March 1963.

It would be true to say that Kilmarnock had had better teams than the one that they had in 2016. Now managed by an amiable Geordie called Lee Clark, they had been lucky to win a play-off final and thus escape relegation in May, but they were not really off to the best of starts this season either. They were also one of the most poorly supported teams in Scotland with swathes of empty seats always on view at Rugby Park, even when they were played Celtic or Rangers.

It is commonly supposed in some Celtic-supporting circles that all Ayrshire supports Rangers. Frankly, this is not true. This seems to stem from Kilmarnock supporters singing 'Hello, hello, we are the Killie boys' (a lot of people think they are singing 'Billy' not 'Killie') and there is a dismal propensity for Kilmarnock to sell their players to Rangers. And they do wear blue! But one of Celtic's greatest ever players – some argue that he was indeed the greatest of them all – Sunny Jim Young, the inspiring right-half and in later years captain of Willie Maley's great pre-war side, was from Kilmarnock. And no one is ever going to convince me that Robert Burns, that man of great humanity and brilliant poetry, would have been a Rangers supporter! He was no great lover of the Presbyterian Kirk, nor the British crown either, come to think of it.

On a more serious note, one often wondered how long Kilmarnock could keep going, particularly when squabbles at boardroom level kept hitting the headlines. Yet, founded in 1869 and the second oldest surviving Scottish senior team, Kilmarnock were very much an integral part of the Scottish football scene.

A gentleman with the name of Souleymane Coulibaly woke Celtic Park up after about 30 minutes of anodyne slumber. Spotting Dorus de Vries off his line, the Ivorian lobbed the ball over his head from about 35 or 40 yards. It was simple, effective and brilliant. The reaction of the Celtic crowd was first stunned, disbelieving silence, then a few curses, then a few questions of the 'Did he really mean that?' variety before a reluctant ripple of applause, and then defiant chanting and singing. Poor Dorus de Vries! He was substituted at half-time, and Craig Gordon was restored. The story was put out that de Vries was injured and unable to continue, but we all suspected that it was merely to spare his feelings.

As far as Celtic were concerned, that piece of brilliance by Coulibaly was almost irrelevant, for three minutes later Celtic were level, then before half-time they were 2–1 ahead with both goals scored by Moussa Dembele. It was a wake-up call that had been heeded! The second half was more or less total one-way traffic. First James Forrest scored after a fine one-two with Tommy Rogic, then Leigh Griffiths, standing on the goal line headed on a Simunovich header, Scott Sinclair then scored with a penalty kick, before Tommy Rogic with a miskick which trickled past the demoralised goalkeeper made it an emphatic 6–1 victory.

This was fine vintage Celtic stuff. It probably did the credibility of Scottish football no good at all, but those who claimed to be experts at Scottish football were already telling people the name of the League winners. It was odd to hear this at the end of September, and in some ways it was unsettling, for it meant that Celtic really had to prove their credentials all winter and to stay at the top. Hearts were second at this point, both Aberdeen and Rangers having proved themselves incapable of getting over the psychological traumata of their Parkhead maulings. Beating Kilmarnock, or anyone else, 6–1 kept up the psychological pressure. It was also good for the fans, who loved every minute of it.

Dens Park, Dundee on 1 October was the next port of call in the Premiership. This followed immediately after the epic 3–3 draw with Manchester City, a performance much praised, and deservedly so, by all concerned, but here used as a rather unconvincing excuse for a Celtic performance at Dens Park. It was indeed a victory, but a considerably less convincing one than the one we had seen last week against Kilmarnock, for example.

It was a fine day at Dens Park for a lunchtime Saturday kick-off to that grand old lady of a stadium, with its rather unique old stand built in 1922 in the shape of an obtuse angle. Those of us of an older vintage had many memories of visiting Dens Park in the great days of Ure and Gilzean in the early 1960s where we, frankly, simply could not get a win for many years. Always unlucky, we felt, but up against a good team who were deservedly League Champions in 1962, and in 1963 had reached the semi-final of the European Cup, some four years before Celtic did!

Happier memories of Celtic performances against Dundee included a magnificent goal scored by John Hughes to qualify Celtic for the League Cup quarter-final in 1965, and a game in midwinter 1967/8 which ended 5–4 for Celtic. Both teams showed a desire to attack, and usually goals came thick and fast. A few weeks before that had been the Scottish League Cup Final of 1967/8 at Hampden (as Celtic were just about to fly out to South America), a great 5–3 win for Celtic, and Dundee being given a great ovation from the magnanimous Celtic crowd as they collected their losers' medals. Their team that day included Jim McLean, in later years to become the misanthropic but successful Manager of Dundee United, the rivals from across the road.

But bad times had settled on Dens Park from the 1970s onwards, with things happening behind the scenes which baffled the press and alienated the fans. Clearly unable to cope with the rise of Dundee United, who had in the 1970s and 1980s been blessed with good progressive management and stewardship (less so now!), Dundee had caused heads to be shaken by repeatedly selling star players and not replacing them since the 1960s onwards, and crazy things always happen when unsavoury characters are allowed to run the show!

Quite a lot of their decent fans had given up, and had been replaced by a somewhat nastier core who waved, for example, flags with vacuous inanities like 'Dundee Derry' on them! Historians and sociologists struggled to cope with and understand that, but there was a residual sadness that such a fine old team had been allowed to decline to such an extent. Now managed by ex-Celt Paul Hartley, there had been a recovery of sorts, but they were still a great deal short of what they could have been, and where their supporters would have liked them to have been, namely up beside Aberdeen, for example.

Dundee, however, can always be relied upon to put up a fight against Celtic especially at home, and this was what happened today. Celtic, for their part, were a little lacklustre but still professional enough to win the game 1–0, thanks to a goal from Scott Brown, of all people, early in the second half when he was on hand to squeeze the ball home following some sustained Celtic pressure.

The Likely Lads: Scott Brown and Kieran Tierney.

A second Celtic goal would have settled everyone but it did not come, and Dundee might, with a bit of luck, have earned themselves an equaliser. Celtic and their fans, both in the ground and watching on TV throughout the world, were relieved to hear the full-time whistle. Two things puzzled the Scottish football fan about this game. Why was there a crowd of only 8,000 there, when there were many empty seats in parts of the ground while it was so difficult for Celtic fans to get a ticket for their own end? Clearly some more joined-up thinking was required here, for the strict attitude to segregation was effectively losing a lot of money. The other source of puzzlement was why could Dundee not play like that every week? They would not have their almost perpetual struggle against relegation if they did!

The season now adjourned for the International break. I am sure that I am not the only Celtic fan in the world who finds these breaks a crashing bore. I am also aware that this is entirely because Scotland do not have a team worthy of the name and haven't done so for the past twenty years. It is really difficult, also (is it not?), to get involved in supporting a team consisting of virtual unknowns from the English Championship who speak with a pronounced English accent and are only playing because their granny came from Peterhead or some place? This 'International break' consisted of an insipid draw with Lithuania at Hampden and a real pumping in Slovakia. The Celtic players involved – Forrest, Griffiths and Tierney – earned pass marks, I suppose, but the empty seats at Hampden for the Lithuania game told their own story. It was a relief to get back to the real football of the following week when Motherwell came to Celtic Park.

Motherwell were now managed by our old friend Mark McGhee, one of those characters of Scottish football who seemed to always be around and who kept coming back in some shape or form. Motherwell, who would in December play the most exciting game of the season against Celtic, were no slouches here either, and they put up some stiff resistance before losing 2–0. They would have reason for feeling a great deal happier about their performance than when they were last at Parkhead in August in the Scottish League Cup, for that was a 0–5 hammering. This one was at least respectable for the claret and ambers.

The result put Celtic four points ahead of second-placed Aberdeen, and it was a regulation, if uninspired, victory for the side. It is a truism that leagues are not always won by champagne football. There are times when one has to grind out victories against dogged opposition who have come to the ground with no ambition any higher than to win a point. Motherwell were compact and well organised, and although they did not really present any great attacking threat, there was always the possibility as the second half wore on, and Celtic were only 1–0 ahead, that they might just sneak an equaliser. The impatience of the fans did not help either.

It was good to see Liam Henderson getting a start in this game. Liam had not perhaps come as far as some would have predicted for him following his blistering start to the game a few seasons ago, but he was still a more than adequate squad player, and was the only member of the squad who had a Scottish Cup medal won in a final against Rangers! He had done this last season when he was on loan with Hibs. He was finding it very difficult to force his way into this Celtic midfield,

Liam Henderson.

which absolutely teemed with talent – Brown, McGregor, Rogic, Armstrong were all very difficult men to displace. Liam had a good game today, however.

It was an unusual game as well, for Celtic were playing in the first half towards the Jock Stein Stand end of the ground, when they normally attack the Lisbon Lions end first. Celtic had gone ahead in the first half when Sinclair scored. It came from a good cross by James Forrest which Moussa Dembele fluffed, but Scott Sinclair was waiting. This was about the 20th minute, and on several other occasions before half-time they might have gone further ahead.

The second half was more of the same, with Kieran Tierney on one occasion charging down the left wing before crashing a shot into the woodwork, a goal that would have been much deserved, and Scott Brown brought a great save out of Craig Samson, but there was no further addition to the score until late in the game when Dembele was pulled down by Craig Samson when there didn't seem to be any great danger. Fortunately, the sensible referee John Beaton did not see fit to send Samson off, but it gave Celtic a penalty which Dembele converted to send Celtic fans home happy and relieved. They would not now play another League game for eleven days, because there was now a 'break' to deal (badly) with Borussia Monchengladbach in the Champions League and (brilliantly) with Rangers in the Scottish League Cup.

It was to Victoria Park, Dingwall, the home of Ross County, that we next turned our attention on Wednesday, 26 October. There are Celtic supporters who tell me that they have not yet been to that distant venue. I would urge them to remedy that deficiency as soon as practicable. One really must hold up one's hands in admiration for that team whose success proves that there is no real excuse for those with a far larger fan base than Ross County but who fail to deliver. Hiding behind the hoary old excuse of 'under the shadow of the Old Firm who steal our supporters' simply will not do. It is manifestly not true, and Ross County have shown the world that on a miniscule budget and with a stadium that holds more than the population of their town (astonishing, but true!), it is possible to compete at the highest level.

Three times in recent years they have beaten Celtic, two of these three times embarrassingly so in a semi-final, and of course in 2016, they went on to win the Scottish League Cup. Their ground is trim and well-appointed, their fans are friendly and welcoming and they have a bus park which believes in letting the buses go as soon possible after the final whistle. They have a good Manager in Jim McIntyre, and apart from one fellow (whom we will come to in April!), their players are a decent bunch.

And it was a fine, crisp autumn Wednesday afternoon for the drive up the A9. Large parts of the Highlands, of course, do not have trees at the best of times, but other parts do, and they were a wonderful mellow sight. 'Come autumn, sae pensive in yellow and grey,' said Robert Burns. It was indeed a wonderful sight. We were, of course, still very upbeat about last Sunday's result against Rangers, and confident that our team, no matter how badly they were doing in Europe, were still a match for whatever Scotland could throw at us.

Celtic's team was a much changed one from Sunday, as Brendan Rodgers took the opportunity to give a few of the 'fringe' players a game, if men like Izaguirre,

McGregor, Henderson and Christie could be called that. The man who really caught the eye that night, however, was Patrick Roberts, who scored in the first three minutes before many of the Celtic fans had managed to get into the ground, and then played a part in Celtic's other three goals which all came in the last 10 minutes.

The goal flurry at the end, which meant a 4–0 victory, tended to distort the picture a little because the game was a great deal closer. But Armstrong, Sinclair and Dembele did the business at the end, and already, with still another game remaining to be played in the month of October, Celtic supporters felt brave enough to shout things like 'Champions', et cetera! Even though Aberdeen had blown up at Hamilton the previous night, and Rangers and Hearts were now generally discounted as challengers, quite a few of us still felt that this was being a little premature! Some felt that Craig Gordon was lucky to escape stronger action than a yellow card when he came out of his goal and knocked over a Ross player with his knee, but it was more of a misjudgement than anything deliberate, and it could not have been a penalty kick for it was well outside the box.

It was late before we got home, but it was well worth the long trip, as we reflected as convoys of Celtic buses roared down the A9. The buses would be required again fairly soon, for on Saturday, Celtic were heading north again, this time to Aberdeen for what promised to be the most difficult game of the season so far. Apart from having a vital bearing on the League, we also now knew that it was a rehearsal for the Scottish League Cup Final in a month's time.

The 12.00 kick-off meant an early start for those going to the game, but it was probably appreciated by those who weren't at Pittodrie, for it would allow them to have the rest of the day to themselves. This was often a pleasant experience if we had won, for we could then sit back and listen to the rest of the games unfolding on TV. SKY TV and BT Sports had commentators who could, occasionally, annoy punters – but that was their job, was it not? - but no one could deny that they did a good job in allowing all supporters to watch the game, even though there was a down side to it all in the way that they were able to dictate kick-off times, and also in their blatant propagation of betting, something which did football (and society in general) few favours.

That, of course, is the subject of a larger discussion, but TV coverage meant that every Celtic supporter anywhere in the world could now, effectively, watch more or less every Celtic game. It meant that we were no longer entirely dependent on the press for information – a sad side-effect of all this being the collapse and death of the Saturday evening paper – and we could make up our own minds about who was playing well for Celtic and who was not.

Very few played badly for Celtic that crisp autumn day of 29 October. Celtic won 1–0, thanks to a fine Tommy Rogic strike into the beach end goal halfway through the first half, when he picked up a loose ball, controlled it with one foot and scored with the other. Thereafter, Celtic controlled the game, not doing anything crazy (other than an ill-advised backward header from Sviatchenko) and generally looking like champions. Aberdeen had a few chances late in the game but so too did Celtic, and the only other memorable (if that is the word) incident was a rather undignified difference of opinion between Scott Brown and Jonny Hayes (you would have guessed it would be these two, wouldn't you?) which saw pushing rather than punching and earned a couple of yellow cards. Inevitably the word 'handbags' was dragged into that one! Lustig also was yellow-carded, as were another three players at different points of the game, but it was never a dirty match.

There have been better Aberdeen v. Celtic games, but that was of little concern to the fans as we headed downwards and homewards. Celtic were now nine points ahead of Aberdeen with a game in hand, and thus October ended with Celtic spending Hallowe'en and then All Saints' Day in Germany, but with a reassurance that on the home front things were progressing quite satisfactorily.

Celtic had only two League fixtures in November. This was because the second week was an International weekend (a disappointing Scotland defeat to England at Wembley) and the last weekend was of course the Scottish League Cup Final. There were also, of course, two European fixtures, but as far as the League was concerned, Celtic continued on their merry way, experiencing little real difficulty in getting the better of Inverness and Kilmarnock.

Inverness remained the only team to have taken League points off Celtic this season, and their Manager Richie Foran with a commendable honesty came to Glasgow on Guy Fawkes Day saying that his team were going to try to defend and frustrate Celtic. He may or may not have used the horrible cliché 'hit them on the break', but if he didn't, that is what he meant. Inverness, apart from their spectacular night in 2000, don't always do well at Celtic Park. This game turned out to be quite typical of so many Celtic v. Inverness encounters in the past.

Rodgers played both Dembele and Griffiths in this game, using the rivalry between the two of them to try to get more goals from each of them, but at half-time, when the score was still 0–0, it did not seem to be working. Celtic's 'three at the back' idea was working well until Lustig was badly injured in a clash with our old friend Josh Meekings, whom we had met in unhappy circumstances at Hampden in the Scottish Cup semi-final of 2015. The hard-working Lustig had to be taken off to be replaced by Izaguirre (Tierney was already out injured). Armstrong then adopted a more defensive role on the right. Still no goal came, and Celtic had one or two fairly glaring misses.

It all changed quite quickly in the second half, though, when the fast-improving Callum McGregor released Scott Sinclair to put Celtic one up. Thereafter it was one-way traffic towards the Jock Stein end, and it was no real surprise when the combination of Dembele and Griffiths struck, Griffiths finishing the job off when Dembele's shot had been parried by Fon Williams. This was bad enough for Inverness, but things got a lot worse when Greg Tansey was sent off for a series of fouls. None of them were all that serious, but there were a lot of them. About 10 minutes after that, Tommy Rogic from a cut-back from Stuart Armstrong made it 3–0, and the game thereafter fizzled out with more than half the crowd away home long before the full-time whistle.

Tommy Rogic scored the last goal, as we have seen, from a Stuart Armstrong pass, and it was Stuart Armstrong who scored the only goal of the next game, getting the ball from a Dembele prod late in the first half to finish the job. The game was very unusual in many respects. It was at Rugby Park, Kilmarnock on a Friday night, 18 November. Fairly obviously it was for TV purposes, and it was a bit of a novelty for Celtic to play at that time, for their TV times tended to be Saturday or Sunday at lunchtime. It was a cold night on the all-weather pitch at Kilmarnock, and Celtic decided for reasons best known to themselves to play in their pink jerseys with black pants. We have grown accustomed to seeing all yellow, all black and now we had pink. None of these strips made Celtic look like Celtic, and although one could perhaps see some sort of a colour clash (although no one had ever done so before) with Kilmarnock's blue and white stripes, why couldn't Celtic wear all-green? Indeed, why couldn't they wear the Hoops?

The answer, of course, lay in commerce. Attempts to sell an all pink Celtic strip would come to naught, if the team did not wear it several times. So a Friday night in November at Kilmarnock, where there would be a lot more people watching on TV than at Rugby Park itself, seemed a good choice to advertise the pink strips, particularly when Christmas was now not all that far away. Nevertheless, one really had to work hard to realise that these fellows in the pink were actually Celtic. One wonders, too, how many of these pink strips were actually sold?

For the first time, Brendan Rodgers gave a start to Dedryck Boyata, who was close to becoming Celtic's forgotten man. Boyata played well alongside Erik Sviatchenko, and after Armstrong scored the goal, although Kilmarnock put up a brave fight particularly towards the end of the game, Celtic were rarely threatened and could indeed have scored more goals. It was another of those games where Celtic, without necessarily being brilliant or spectacular, nevertheless did the job.

For someone who did not understand the dynamics of the Scottish game, this would have been a strange experience. The Celtic crowd was accommodated at both ends and both stands were packed (why, incidentally, do Kilmarnock call their stands names like 'Moffat' and 'Chadwick'? Have they never heard of Frank Beattie or Davie Sneddon or Matta Smith?), whereas the pitiful Kilmarnock crowd were in the main stand and in the stand opposite, both of them with swathes of empty seats. This sort of thing is just plain stupid, in that it does them out of a great deal of money when there were Celtic supporters in abundance who would have filled the stands for them. It does no favours for the image of Scottish football either, and one often wonders how teams like Kilmarnock survive, when they fail to grasp opportunities. The pies are indeed good, however!

Christmas was approaching, as we have said, and the Celtic crowd, ever inventive and innovative, had a new song about the new Manager. Last Christmas, apparently, they gave their heart to the lady/gentleman of their life who discarded the offer 'the very next day'. This Christmas they were not going to be anything like so stupid for they were going to give their heart to Brendan Rodgers, a man who pronounced himself happy with tonight's result. Celtic had slipped up at Rugby Park in the past, and it was always nice to get an away win of any kind. And it being a Friday night, the weekend had not even really started!

CHAPTER **EIGHT**
THE SCOTTISH LEAGUE CUP

The Scottish League Cup is probably, in fact definitely, Celtic's least favourite domestic trophy. At the start of the 2016/17 campaign, Celtic had won the trophy fifteen times, as distinct from Rangers' twenty-seven. Granted, both Celtic and Rangers are miles ahead of anyone else, but as Rangers will always be the yardstick against whom Celtic are measured, the disparity was considered unacceptable by Celtic supporters who were in any way historically minded.

There were many reasons for this disparity. Celtic had been slow starters in this tournament (which only began after World War Two), and it was as late as Hallowe'en 1956 before we registered our first success after a decade of striving. We were slow starters in another sense as well, in that we were prone to start the season badly, and this tournament was usually played at the beginning of the season. Celtic repeatedly failed to qualify from the sectional stage, but Rangers, after starting the tournament well in the first few years, did similarly badly and teams like Motherwell, Dundee, Hearts and particularly East Fife did well. Incredible though it seems, the Fifers had won the trophy three times before Celtic even appeared in a final!

Then there was a run in the 1970s when we lost in finals, sometimes because we underestimated our opponents, sometimes because we took our eye off the ball because of European commitments, and sometimes in bizarre circumstances, e.g., December 1973, when referee Bobby Davidson sanctioned play on a pitch that was manifestly unplayable in the opinion of quite a few journalists and spectators. Other times we simply had sheer bad luck.

But the real damage came in the 1980s and 1990s, when Celtic went from December 1982 until November 1997 without winning the trophy. Most of these years coincided with the 'biscuit tin' days of the Kelly regime. Celtic occasionally had bad luck in finals then as well – losing to Rangers in extra time, for example, on two occasions, or to Raith Rovers in a penalty shoot-out – but it was an era where Rangers took full advantage of our weakness and mismanagement and the phrase 'When the cat's away, the mice will play' came to mind, as did 'For evil to triumph all that is necessary for good men to do nothing'. It is sadly true that if Celtic do not stand up to Rangers, no one else will either. These were grim times, certainly as far as the Scottish League Cup was concerned.

Since the turn of the century, Celtic's League Cup performances have improved with wins in 2000, 2001, 2006, 2009 and 2015. Historically, there were also the great days of the five-in-a-row from 1965/66 until 1969/70, and the much commemorated 7–1 victory over Rangers in October 1957, and I personally have two other favourites. The 1997/98 win over Dundee United finally removed the inferiority complex of the 1990s, and showed us that we could win trophies. Had we not won the trophy that year, we might not have won the League in 1998 and that would have been catastrophic. And then, talking about catastrophes, the 2000 League Cup win over an equally stricken Aberdeen side (whose supporters were also suffering terribly from poor management) came in the wake of our Inverness Caledonian Thistle disgrace in the Scottish Cup a month previously. Our victory over the Dons, fitful and unimpressive though it might have been, gave us at least something towards the regaining of our self-respect, and put a smile back on our faces for at least one weekend.

The Scottish League Cup started life in World War Two as the Southern League Cup. There was no Scottish Cup in the war years and the Southern League (a wartime organisation doing the job of the Scottish League which, along with the SFA, had virtually disappeared) thought that this Southern League Cup might perform the same function as the Scottish Cup had done. As Celtic had a chronically dreadful team during World War Two, we never won the Southern League Cup.

Then this same trophy was renamed the Scottish League Cup and played for from season 1946/47 onwards to supplement the existing tournaments, as both Division 'A' and Division 'B' had only sixteen teams and therefore not enough League fixtures. The tournament proved an immediate success, and although it has never really rivalled the grand old lady called the Scottish Cup (which has been going since 1873/74!), it has nevertheless proved a valuable addition to the season, and teams like East Fife, Partick Thistle, Raith Rovers, Livingston and Ross County have all had their moments of glory (regrettably often at Celtic's expense!). This has to be good for the game in general but Celtic's record, although containing, as we have seen, many great deeds, has also seen some horrors. Those of us who recall the 'headless chickens' defending of the 1971/72 final against Partick Thistle or could share the agony of Paul McStay against Raith Rovers in 1994/95 will testify to that.

The Scottish League Cup can also claim a success in spawning its English equivalent from 1961 onwards, but it has also suffered some terrible things from people who claim to have its best interests at heart. For one thing, it has been a sitting duck for sponsorship. Sponsorship may well pump some much needed money into the game, but the price has been that the Scottish League Cup has had to change its name to the name of some lager, a soft drink and now, heaven help us, the name of a betting firm. This does the tournament no favours at all, and your writer will call the trophy nothing other than the Scottish League Cup, or perhaps League Cup for short. A Raith Rovers fan once boasted to me that his team had beaten Celtic in 1994/95 in the tournament that he called by the name of a soft drink. He was taken aback by my reply, which was that if he called the tournament by that name, people would assume that it was a pre-season Mickey Mouse kind of nonsense rather than a genuine national Scottish competition, in which not only Celtic but also teams like Aberdeen, Rangers and Hearts had participated.

But the other piece of devaluation came in the shape of the permanent chopping and changing of the format. From virtually its start until the early 1970s, the League Cup started the season a sectional format, the winners of a four-team section went on to the quarter final, and the whole tournament was completed by late October every year. This was successful. And what a feeling it was to approach Christmas with its cold weather and general hysteria knowing that there was one trophy on the sideboard! This was true of 1956, 1957, 1965, 1966, 1967 and 1969, for example,

But then greed took over. Two teams got to qualify and when Celtic and Rangers found themselves in a now seeded group of Celtic, Rangers, Arbroath and East Fife, it was not too difficult to predict which two it would be! After a couple of years of this, it was changing time again, and now to a straight knockout, something that would continue with the odd change now and again until 2016. The dithering revealed itself in the date of the final. Until about 2000, the final tended to be played before New Year, including in 1973, in the game already mentioned, the final being played on the ludicrous date of 13 December! They got the weather and the attendance they deserved for that! But after 2000, the final was played in the more sensible month of March, and the tournament gained in prestige as a result.

'If it ain't broke, don't fix it,' is always a sensible maxim, but a revolutionary change took place in summer 2016. The tournament returned to a sectional format, but was played in the month of July in the erroneous belief that it would attract bigger crowds. The four teams who were playing in Europe – Celtic, Aberdeen, Hearts and Hibs, this year, were exempt from this stage of the tournament, and Celtic played their first game against Motherwell at Celtic Park on Wednesday, 10 August in what was the round of the last sixteen. Twelve teams had qualified from the eight sectional groups of five each (eight winners and the four best runners-up) to join the European representatives, although that was by now a misnomer, for only Celtic remained in Europe!

The sectional stages had contained a new innovation. If the game was drawn, there was no extra time but an immediate penalty shoot-out for a point for the winners of the shoot-out. (Still three points if you won the game in normal time.) This looked like a gimmick, and a rather amateurish one at that, but it was what the Scottish League had decided. (To be fair, it did bring a little excitement now and again.) No such nonsense in the knockout stage. There would indeed be a penalty shoot-out to decide the winners, but after extra time.

Extra time was not required at Celtic Park, however. Celtic had finished the previous season by taking seven goals off Motherwell in glorious sunshine before the League Championship trophy was presented. This was more or less a continuation, for the result was 5–0. There were several differences, of course, in personnel and in weather, but particularly, and rather sadly, in attendance, for there were little more than 20,000 present. The stands were depressingly empty.

It is often disappointing to see such low attendances at Celtic Park for what I have always considered to be important games. There are several reasons, of course. One is that it is midweek which creates problems for supporters from very far away – Ireland, north of Scotland and England (yet that does not always prevent them attending midweek European games), the game is not usually included in the Season Ticket package which means that you have to pay, and distressingly often you hear the 'I've given them enough money' sort of pseudo-supporter.

In this case, also, the opposition were Motherwell, a team with no great support themselves and with no great pedigree in the Scottish League Cup, which they had won once as far back as 1950/51 and appeared in the final on only two other occasions. Only to an extent can one blame TV coverage. TV coverage is great when Celtic are playing at Ibrox, Tynecastle, Pittodrie or some other ground where there are simply not enough tickets to go round. Being at the game is always so much more memorable, even though BT Sport coverage with the excellent, controversial but very pro-Celtic Chris Sutton, was first class.

One always fears that with a poor crowd, something of the zip goes out of Celtic's performance, and one recalls with horror the game in autumn 2013 when Celtic exited the Scottish League Cup before a minuscule crowd in a dreadful performance against Morton, a performance which was not helped by the lack of atmosphere. Most of the noise that night came from the small knot of Morton supporters who were enjoying their night out in the big, but empty, stadium. Celtic supporters stand condemned for that one and I feared that something similar might just happen tonight against Motherwell.

My fears were, however, unjustified, and the 30,000 Celtic fans who chose to absent themselves that night missed a real treat, for this was the night that the newcomers, Sinclair and Dembele, showed that they were fitting in well, and that we really did have a splendid team beginning to develop at Celtic Park. The team knitted splendidly together, and had it not been for an inspired performance in the Motherwell goal from Craig Samson, the score might well have been double figures.

It was Scott Sinclair's first start for the club and the Parkhead crowd's first opportunity to see him, and he was good, but the man who really impressed was Tom Rogic, whose first goal of his two was a thundering volley. Moussa Dembele also scored twice (once from the penalty spot) and Sinclair marked his appearance and the start of his rapport with the home fans with a fine goal. Brendan Rodgers felt able to give two of his youngsters, Tony Ralston and Jamie McCart, a run near the end in the same way that Jock Stein would often 'blood' his Quality Street kids like Danny McGrain and Kenny Dalglish in similar games. The support left Celtic Park that night full of praise and optimism for the future, while Mark McGhee, the Manager of Motherwell, was honest enough to admit that 'we were outclassed'.

Celtic thus joined Aberdeen, Rangers, St Johnstone, Dundee United, Morton, Queen of the South and Alloa in the quarter-finals, the draw for which was held at Celtic Park immediately after this game. The draw was unseeded, but still managed to produce home ties for Celtic, Rangers and Aberdeen with Alloa Athletic having the honour of a trip to Celtic Park, and the closest-looking tie of the round being that at Pittodrie between Aberdeen and St Johnstone.

Alloa Athletic are one of the grand old teams of Scottish football. Founded as early as 1878, they play at Recreation Park, now sadly called the Indodrill Stadium when Recreation Park would have done just as well! Inevitably a small team in what is called the 'wee County' of Clackmannanshire, they have, nevertheless, had their moments in Scottish football, having won the Scottish League Second Division in 1922. Their first game of the 1922/23 season was against Celtic, and Willie Maley, Chairman of the Scottish League, was invited to unfurl their flag for them. They have yet to appear in any national final.

In recent years they have had their moments, good and bad. In 2015, they had earned promotion to the Championship after a rather lucky win over Forfar in the play-offs, but they were clearly not ready for this step and finished up last with only three wins in season 2015/16. Consequently, they were back in Division One, but now this year they had made a good start under a young and enthusiastic Manager called Jack Ross, a man who interviewed well. They played in yellow and black and were nicknamed the 'wasps' or the 'hornets'.

It would have been a titanic shock to everyone's system if Alloa had achieved anything against Celtic, but there were times when we began to wonder. The context was an empty Celtic Park with a crowd considerably fewer than the 20,000 who had been there for the Motherwell game in the previous round – 16,000 was given, and even that may have been an exaggeration. In any case, it looked bad when compared with Rangers the night before. They had attracted 26,000 to see them demolish Queen of the South 5–0. Celtic had not had a good week. Hammered mercilessly in Barcelona last midweek, and having dropped a couple of points at Inverness at the weekend, this was a crucial game for Celtic. And of course, we were all haunted by the spectres of previous failures against smaller teams, notably Morton in this same tournament three years ago.

It was not an easy 'watch' this equinox night of 21 September. Fortunately, Brendan Rodgers had resisted the temptation to 'rest' players, something that disrespects the tournament and insults your opponents. When teams in England do this, they frequently get the outcome that their arrogance deserves. So it was Celtic's best men who were hammering away at the Alloa goal that night, but they were constantly frustrated by a well organised side who were well supported by their small but loyal band of followers, and were growing in confidence the longer the game went on.

One moment, just before half-time, caused a certain amount of embarrassment when Craig Gordon was given a yellow card for a high tackle of Greg Spence of Alloa. It was outside the box, so there would be no penalty, but Celtic Park was relieved to see the colour yellow rather than red from referee Alan Muir, when there could have been no real complaint if it had been red. It was described by

John Barnes on the BBC website as a 'kung fu' style kick, and even Chris Sutton on BT Sport described it as 'appalling' and 'endangering an opponent'. Basically, Craig was a very lucky man. A similar thing would happen at Dingwall in a few weeks' time, but this one was worse.

Craig Gordon, fine goalkeeper that he is, has a tendency to be rash at times and he certainly was here. He was at this point of the season fighting for his place, and indeed had only won it back this very night, for Dorus De Vries had been in the goal at Inverness at the weekend. He and Celtic have a lot to be grateful to referee Alan Muir for. The season might have been a lot different, if Mr Muir had reacted differently.

More immediately, half-time came and went with still no goal for Celtic and the forwards prodigal of chances. Patrick Roberts was having a particularly and uncharacteristically bad night, the Alloa defence having sussed that he had no right foot. He was substituted by Scott Sinclair, but this brought no immediate improvement. Celtic continued to press, but the Alloa defence held out and we were beginning to reckon on the possibility of extra time. We kept waiting for the part-timers to tire and allow Celtic to score, but it still wouldn't happen.

It was within the last 10 minutes when James Forrest made ground by running across the goal and then firing home from about 18 yards. The cry was not so much one of acclamation as of relief, for now the part-timers really were exhausted, and in any case Moussa Dembele, with a fine piece of play, added a second just before the 90 minutes.

It would be a fair statement that Celtic, for all their dominance and pressure, 'got away with one' that night. It was hard to argue in favour of Craig Gordon's tackle, something that got worse and worse the more one saw of it on TV playbacks, and there had been a disturbing lack of penetration in the forward play. But the important thing was that Celtic were through to join Rangers and Morton, and then Aberdeen beat St Johnstone the following night. The draw was made immediately after that game, and all the clever dicks who 'knew all along' that it was all meant to be an Old Firm final, had to eat their words when Celtic and Rangers were drawn against each other. Aberdeen would play Morton on Saturday, 22 October at Hampden, and Celtic took on Rangers the following day, both with an early kick-off.

The two had, of course, met at an equivalent stage of the Scottish League Cup Final two years previously, and it had been a 2–0 win for Celtic with goals from Chris Commons and Leigh Griffiths. The difference was that Rangers were now back in the Premier Division, but given the state of form of the two clubs, it was difficult to see past Celtic as winners. But then again, form counts for very little between these two teams.

Historically, it would have to be said that in the League Cup, Rangers had the upper hand over Celtic. In the twenty-first century, there had been several clashes in the Scottish League Cup and we recalled with pleasure the League Cup Final of 2009 when Aiden McGeady, who had frequently failed to live up to his promise but had done so that day, scoring a penalty kick in the last minute of injury time after Darren O'Dea, of all people, had put Celtic in front with a header.

It had been St Valentine's Day 2012 when Nemesis, the Greek Goddess who punishes the wicked, had caught up with Rangers and sent them into administration. The business side of the club's history frankly defies analysis, but we know that in 2012/13 they played in Division 2, 2013/14 in Division 1, 2014/15 in the Championship but they stayed there because they failed to gain promotion in a play-off. They had better luck in season 2015/16, and now they were back. Some Celtic supporters might talk about 'Sevco' and 'Newco', but they looked awfully like the old Rangers to me!

Clearly this game meant a great deal to Rangers, but no more than it did to Celtic. It would be true to say that as Celtic supporters made their way to Hampden, our season was 'teetering' on the brink. Wednesday night had seen a performance from a lacklustre Celtic team which had silenced and shocked everyone. This had been against Borussia Monchengladbach in the Champions League at Celtic Park, and there was little doubt that a repeat performance would inflict all sorts of agonies on the support, who had hitherto been very loyal to Brendan Rodgers, but who might turn against him, as they had done with Ronnie Deila. It would also mean that there could be no treble.

Those of us of little faith were duly upbraided by the rest who pointed out the undeniable fact that Borussia were of a different class altogether from Rangers, and that on any rational analysis Celtic would defeat Rangers. It promised to be a great occasion, however, as Celtic and Rangers games often were. It would be remembered, one way or other, for a very long time indeed.

But before that game could be played, there was the other semi-final between Aberdeen and Morton, and it was one which raised a serious question about the wisdom of playing such games at Hampden, for the crowd was a paltry 16,000. There were reasons for that, the main one being that the game was live on television, added to the undeniable fact that it was not cheap to get in. Neutral support more or less did not exist at Hampden, Morton's support was vocal but small and the Aberdeen Red Army could hardly be blamed for not turning up in huge numbers. The game was played at lunchtime, something that would have necessitated a very early start from Aberdeen, and the temptation to stay in the Granite City and meet with one's friends in the pub to watch it must have been a strong one. It was more or less impossible to get from Aberdeen to Hampden for kick-off time, if you were relying on public transport!

One cannot help thinking that if the game had been played at McDiarmid Park or Tannadice, the crowd might have been, of necessity, even smaller than 16,000, but the ground would have been packed and the atmosphere would have been quite something. The game as a result would have been that much better. And the game would have still been on TV, so no one would have missed the opportunity of seeing the game. As it was, the empty seats did not do the image of Scottish football any good, and Celtic supporters were right to raise the question of why Aberdeen would get over 20,000 tickets for the final, when even with the addition of Morton supporters, only 16,000 were at the semi?

Jim Duffy's Morton in fact put up a strong fight, but it was the Dons who got the goals at the right time through Rooney in the second half when a shock result looked a possibility, and then Kenny McLean confirmed the Aberdeen victory at the end. Morton had had their moments as well, but it was the Dons who triumphed.

There was no problem about filling Hampden for the other semi-final on the Sunday. There had been some rain earlier in the day, but the game was played in pleasant autumn sunshine. Dembele and Sinclair played up front for Celtic with Griffiths on the bench, while the back four was a very strong-looking Lustig, Simunovich, Sviatchenko and Tierney. Brown, Forrest, Bitton and Rogic were the midfielders with McGregor, Armstrong and Roberts on the bench.

The game kicked off with Celtic attacking the Mount Florida end, and as always in such games, the pace was relentless and possibly a little more impressive than the quality of the action on view. The referee was Craig Thomson, a man who courted controversy, one felt, but also not a man to duck a difficult decision. He would make two crucial decisions in this game, both in front of the Celtic end. One was correct and the other wrong.

His correct one fooled the crowd and the TV commentators. Barry McKay collapsed like a sack of potatoes following a tackle from Jozo Simunovich. 'Penalty,' shouted the red, white and blue gentlemen and ladies at the far end, 'Penalty,' said the commentators, and our hearts sank when Craig Thomson seemed to be pointing at the spot. The Celtic defenders for a horrible moment thought likewise. In fact, he was pointing to award a free kick to Celtic and then to book McKay for diving. TV playbacks proved that he was right.

He was less correct in the early minutes of the second half. In the aftermath of a Celtic corner on the left, Scott Sinclair sent over a lovely cross and Erik Sviatchenko rose to head home. It looked a lovely goal, but Rangers defender Clint Hill had gone down. If anything, it looked as if Hill was trying to foul Sviatchenko rather than the other way round, and the disallowing of this goal was a clear injustice.

Celtic remained on top throughout the second half. Scott Sinclair hit the bar with a free kick, and several other Celtic attempts came close, but Rangers were not out of it. They were playing a great deal better than they had at Parkhead a month ago, and there was in any case the fear that they could run up and score. Griffiths and Armstrong were now on for Celtic, but still Rangers with their goalkeeper Matt Dilks in inspirational (and lucky) form held out. We were just beginning to reconcile ourselves to the thought of extra time and possible penalties (we recalled with numbing intensity the Scottish Cup semi-final of six months before) when Celtic struck.

It was a long ball out of defence from Simunovich which found Griffiths. He made space down the right and crossed for Moussa Dembele to score what was his fourteenth goal of the season. Everyone then ran to the supporters at the right corner flag (as seems to be the wont after goals at Hampden these days), and joyous were the celebrations, especially when Craig Thomson blew for full time a few minutes later.

It was only after we got home and the goal was replayed countless times that we realised that Dembele had done what was known as a 'rabona' and the goal was scored by Dembele's back foot. He might have scored in any case if he had used his front foot, but it showed his cleverness of touch and awareness of where

Moussa Dembele (hidden) scores the goal that beats Rangers.

the ball actually was. It had put Celtic into their thirty-first League Cup Final to play Aberdeen on Sunday, 27 November at Hampden.

It was Aberdeen's fourteenth Scottish League Cup Final and they had won six of them – in 1955/56 against St Mirren, 1976/77 against Celtic, 1985/86 against Hibs, 1989/90 against Rangers, 1995/96 against Dundee and 2013/14 against Inverness Caledonian Thistle. Celtic and Aberdeen had met only twice in a League Cup Final and it was one victory for each club. Celtic's had been in 2000 when we were at a low ebb and needed something, and Aberdeen's had been in 1976/77, a mockery of a game in which Celtic had all the play but could not score, and Aberdeen had scored early in extra time and held on. In the long and lamentable catalogue of Celtic League Cup Final defeats, this one had been one of the hardest to take.

Both teams had won the trophy in the last three years. Aberdeen had done so at Celtic Park in 2014, beating Inverness in a penalty shoot-out after a dull 120 minutes, whereas Celtic had won the trophy in 2015 by getting the better of a poor Dundee United side with a degree of ease. Ross County had been the winners the previous year in 2016.

The significance of this trophy was that it was a tangible piece of evidence. A Celtic victory would raise our total to sixteen and be a first step towards a treble, whereas if Aberdeen won, it would be proof that they were a strong force and here to stay. The smart money, however, was on Celtic, who had defeated Aberdeen twice in League games. Celtic were undefeated in Scotland so far this season, yet it was felt that if anyone were to beat them, it would be Aberdeen, who had some fine players in Jonny Hayes, Adam Rooney and Niall McGinn.

Much was made of the fact that Celtic were going for their 100th trophy – 47 Scottish Leagues, 36 Scottish Cups and 15 Scottish League Cups – oh, and one European Cup made a total of 99. Some Celtic historians would have liked to have added the Coronation Cup of 1953 and the Empire Exhibition trophy of 1938, but this was no time to quibble. What was important for the happiness of the Celtic family was a win at Hampden on Sunday, 27 November 2016.

Celtic were without Kieran Tierney, out with an injury for some time, but they had a more than adequate replacement in Emilio Izaguirre, a man much loved by the Celtic faithful. The Honduran was not as good as Tierney, and had a few deficiencies in his play, notably his tendency to beat a few men, make space – and then to blast the ball wildly across the face of goal, hoping for the best – but he was whole-hearted and never gave up. Sinclair was also missing, and Aberdeen must have taken heart from those two absentees.

Other than that, the team was more or less what many of the supporters would have predicted. The weather was not bad for November, still not desperately cold, but a little on the dull side and, although not everyone is a great fan of Hampden Park, nevertheless the lights made a fine sight as we headed towards the ground. The game was all-ticket, but rather surprisingly, a few tickets were being offered for both ends, although only a few. Both sets of supporters were in good voice as the game began.

One of the features of the new Celtic team that had emerged this year was its ability and willingness to find space and to shoot. Previous Celtic teams had been guilty of trying to walk the ball into the net and consequently, they lacked penetration. Surprisingly, the Aberdeen defence did not wise up to this Celtic penchant for shooting from a distance, and by half-time Celtic were 2–0 up with such goals. Tom Rogic scored first from a ball out of defence, and then we had the strange sight of James Forrest running for a distance with the ball and not being challenged before scoring what was a brilliant individual goal – but the Aberdeen fans behind that Mount Florida goal were quite entitled to ask where their defenders were.

Half-time therefore saw the Celtic end in undignified uproar, with only the pessimists among us worried in case of an Aberdeen fightback. Indeed, there was from Aberdeen a fightback of sorts in the early stages of the second half, when they might have scored, but Celtic's strong defence rode out the storm which was indeed more of a hysterical, 'boot the ball forward' nature rather than any well-thought-out plan of action. Aberdeen's key men, Hayes and Rooney, never really got going and both were substituted before the end.

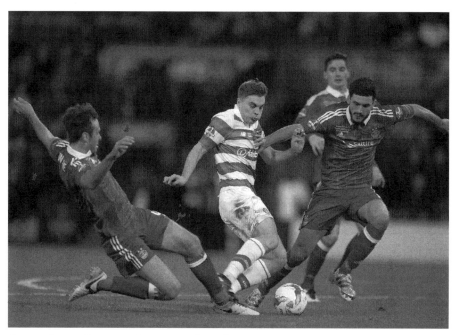

James Forrest scores the second goal.

Moussa Dembele sinks the penalty to put Celtic 3–0 up.

Celtic went further ahead just a minute or two before the normal celebration of Lisbon 67 with the mobile phone lights. O'Connor needlessly brought down James Forrest, and Moussa Dembele slotted home the resultant penalty as he had done so often already this season. Effectively, that was that, and the game gradually fizzled out with any chance of an Aberdeen fightback now gone, and the game finished with a lot of the desolate Aberdeen supporters already sitting on their buses waiting, some impatiently, some resignedly, for the officious stewards to let them begin their long journey home.

It was Celtic's 100th trophy and our 16th Scottish League Cup. More significantly, perhaps, it was the first for Brendan Rodgers. His managerial career in England, although successful, had not exactly been trophy-laden, and it was clear that he relished holding the Scottish League Cup. Green and white ribbons always look nice on silverware, and we headed back to our buses reckoning that there was very little wrong with the world. Thus 1956/57, 1957/78, 1965/66, 1966/7, 1967/68, 1969/69, 1969/70, 1974/75, 1982/83, 1997/98, 1999/2000, 2000/01, 2005/06, 2008/09, 2014/15 were joined by 2016/17 as years in which Celtic won the Scottish League Cup.

It was, as Neil Lennon or Winston Churchill might have said, not the end. It was a springboard to further success as well as being a notable triumph in its own right. For all sorts of reasons, we now had a crowded December to face. December is in many ways the least suitable month for football, according to some. I beg to differ, and certainly December 2016, containing as it did nine fixtures, basically put Celtic in an impregnable position as far as the League was concerned.

CHAPTER **NINE**
A BUSY DECEMBER

Not everyone likes December and Christmas. Everyone, even the most passionate devotees of Christmas, agrees that it can be overdone at times. It seems to start from early November and is an ever-present in many lives with all sorts of things added like Black Friday, the last day, they tell you, that you can get your presents cheap. Brawls and mini-riots have been known to break out on such occasions!

But there are other reasons for not liking December. The weather is usually cold – it certainly was in 2010 – but even if it is not cold it is certainly sunless and dark, and quite a lot of people are prepared to admit that they suffer from SAD – Seasonal Affective Disorder. But what better antidote could there be to that problem than a severe dose of football, especially when played by an excellent team? Celtic in fact played nine games in December. One was the Manchester City game which was now, sadly, a glorified friendly, but the others were League games in which Celtic, without playing brilliantly, nevertheless made everyone more and more convinced, if there ever was any real doubt, that they were going to win the League.

Because of the silly pre-season tournament in which Celtic were allowed to compete at the expense of a League game, and because, more honourably, of the progress in the Scottish League Cup, Celtic in fact had to play Partick Thistle and Hamilton twice each in December, home and away. There were also home games against Dundee and Ross County, an away trip to Motherwell – and, oh yes, a trip to Ibrox on Hogmanay. Some local politicians tried to complain (unconvincingly) that this game should be re-dated on the grounds of fear of disturbances. The truth was that there was no day of the 365 in the year on which anyone could guarantee a trouble-free Old Firm game, if not at the ground itself, certainly in some of the thousands of pubs in Scotland (and indeed the world) where the game would be shown. Celtic fans, from an early stage of the season, were singing confidently to the tune of 'Jingle Bells' what they were going to do to the currant buns on 31 December:

Jingle bells, jingle bells

Jingle all the way

Oh, what fun it is

To F*** the H*** on Hogmanay!

There was no game for Celtic in the midweek immediately following the Scottish League Cup Final success, so we were permitted a 'bask' not in the sun, but in the darkness of impending winter. It was good to have a break in a way and to analyse the season so far. Clearly, with one trophy now wearing green and white ribbons, and with the team well clear in the League, the season had been, so far, a success. New signings Scott Sinclair and Moussa Dembele had shown Brendan Rodgers' perspicacity in the transfer market, but more significant than that had been the clear and obvious improvement in several players since the start of the season. James Forrest was now playing with far more confidence and verve, Stuart Armstrong was a revelation in midfield, Callum McGregor was now far more obvious on the park, where in the past he had occasionally disappeared, and Scott Brown was now back to his combative best. And there was Patrick Roberts as well, potentially the best player of the lot.

The defence had now settled down with Simunovich and Sviatchenko looking secure and in Kieran Tierney there was clearly something special. But the most obvious change that Rodgers had made was in the demeanour of the supporters. The depression, the 'not renewing season ticket', the 'not coming back' rubbish of last year had all gone, and there was the rare feeling of happiness and optimism. Celtic supporters are notoriously hard to please – in my time, I have seen and heard them turn on Jimmy Johnstone, Kenny Dalglish and Paul McStay among others – 'that Henrik Larsson just disnae hae it' they said after his first two games! – but in winter 2016 there was the odd feeling of contentment. They now all looked forward to the next game. Mind you, they had not yet been put to the test. Would they turn on Rodgers if things started to go wrong?

The only minus mark on the pre-Christmas report card was Europe. We had qualified for the sectional stages, and that was good, but the performances after that had been less than totally satisfactory. Two creditable draws (the other game still to be played in Manchester would also be a draw), two defeats from Barcelona, one of which had an embarrassing scoreline, and that strange and feckless performance against Borussia at Celtic Park – so far, the one really bad game of the season in which we certainly underperformed in comparison with our potential – but we reckoned that, in European terms, we were still a work in progress, and that next year would be a great deal better.

One is often very suspicious of the school of thought which says that being out of one competition allows you to concentrate and do better in the others. That is often just an excuse, and is not true anyway. But there may have been some justification for it in the circumstances of this season. A young team, a new Manager, an expectant and revivified support – maybe, it was just as well that we did not get bogged down in Europe this year. We had one stage of the domestic treble. Time now to concentrate on the other two.

Arguably the best game of the season, from a spectator's point of view, was played at Fir Park on 3 December with a lunchtime kick-off. Those who peeled off, as it were, from the family Christmas shopping to find a pub to watch this game did themselves a treat, for it was thrill-a-minute stuff with Celtic possibly lucky to get all three points. Only the most churlish would deny that Motherwell deserved something out of the game.

Fir Park, Motherwell is a grand old stadium. However, until one actually goes to the ground and gets a seat behind the goal, one does not realise that the pitch has a considerable slope running not from one goal to the other but from one side running towards the Main Stand. It is considerable, and the TV cameras do not always make this clear. It is doubtful, however, whether the slope had any effect on the result today, but both teams deserve praise for producing such a great game of football.

It was a ground that had seen some remarkable Celtic performances, both good and bad over the years. We sustained our biggest ever League defeat there in 1937, losing 0–8 in a Friday night game that did not matter for we had won the Scottish Cup the week before, and the players were about to embark on an overnight sleeper train to see the English Cup final between Sunderland and Preston North End. In 1976 in the Scottish Cup we had been 2–0 up at half-time, then blew up completely in the second half. And, of course, there were the recent events of Black Sunday in May 2005 – still, twelve years later, too painful to be recalled.

Happier days had been the winning of the Scottish League in 1966 and a devastating massacre of Motherwell to the tune of 7–0 in September 1982. Generally speaking, one got a good game between these two teams, for they both had a tradition of playing excellent football. Motherwell had produced some excellent players, but tended to sell them on, not least to Celtic. One thinks, for example, of Joe McBride, Dixie Deans and Andy Walker.

Celtic were perhaps aware, as well, that the supporters of Rangers and Aberdeen would be watching them, for their two teams were playing at Ibrox later that afternoon. Rangers' 2–1 victory was actually a good result for Celtic, in that it increased Celtic's lead over Aberdeen, their main challengers. But everyone must have been impressed with Celtic that day, for they seemed to be dead and buried at half-time and yet came back to win triumphantly 4–3.

We learned things about two Celtic players that day. One was that Stuart Armstrong, who was outstanding, particularly in the second half, had developed and was now a very complete player – able to take goals, an incisive passer of the ball and fast runner. Less happily, we now began to ask questions about Kolo Toure. All three goals scored by Motherwell went over his head and there were times when he looked all at sea. And Celtic were still missing Kieran Tierney.

Once again, we had the phenomenon of tickets at a premium for the packed Celtic end with some changing hands at more than the cost price, while the rest of the ground had more than a little elbow room, and even at that, there were more than a few 'fifth columnists' in the Motherwell stands – people who were dressed in 'mufti', i.e. wearing the colours of neither club, and who forgot themselves when Celtic scored at the end! Once again, we must address the question of provincial clubs – 'When will they ever learn?' It certainly seems odd to find clubs claiming that they cannot compete with teams like Celtic on the financial front, and yet refusing money from them! All they need to do is re-draw the segregation areas a little more realistically!

Celtic did not start well that day at Motherwell, and by half-time it was beginning to look as if we were heading for our first defeat of the season. Louis Moult scored in the third minute with a volley from the edge of the penalty box when a long ball had evaded Kolo Toure. Then the second goal came about half an hour later. This was also a volley, but the ball came from the left from Ross McLean (possibly the Motherwell man fouled Mikael Lustig before he crossed) and Moult finished the job at the far post as the serried ranks of Celtic fans behind the goal became quiet and introverted.

Celtic had offered very little at the other end, and it looked for all the world as if the first domestic defeat of the season was forthcoming. But this is Celtic we are talking about. Emilio Izaguirre had gone off injured in the first half and had been replaced by Callum McGregor. Now it was McGregor who brought Celtic back into the game. He did this three minutes into the second half, following a fine one-two with Stuart Armstrong.

The atmosphere at the ground and in pubs and homes changed instantly. Everyone now sat up and took notice, and following another 20 minutes of great football from both sides, Celtic equalised. Stuart Armstrong charged down the left and his cross found the head of Patrick Roberts. Roberts may have been a young man, but he showed all the tactical and practical awareness in the world by heading the ball down into the ground and into the net, when it would have been very easy to head straight at the goalkeeper or put the ball over the bar.

That made it 2–2, and then we had goals in quick succession at each end to make in 3–3. First Lionel Ainsworth was on the right spot to take advantage of a cross from the left, but scarcely had the celebrations died down, when Stuart Armstrong scored a really brilliant goal from a long ball from Patrick Roberts. He shot on the turn and the ball was in the back of the net before anyone knew it. It was 3–3, and what a game!

Everyone might have settled for that, but then enter Tommy Rogic, the Australian who had a tendency to disappear for a spell, and then score a vital goal. How did one pronounce his middle-European name? Did it rhyme with the English word 'logic' or was it more like 'rogish'? Not that it mattered, for the Wizard of Oz produced neither his first nor his last piece of magic in the 90th minute with a shot from the edge of the box, and Celtic had all three points. We were a little sorry for Motherwell and Mark McGhee, but we now knew that this Celtic side never gave up. The momentum of the League Cup victory the previous week had stayed with us, and more and more we found the supporters and the players turning up expecting to win. That is the mark of champions.

There followed the trip to Manchester from where the team returned with a degree of credit, but then it was Firhill for thrills on the night of Friday, 9 December. Partick Thistle are a team that it is hard to dislike. They have never really been strong enough to be anything other than Glasgow's third force, but are proud of their role in serving the diverse community of Maryhill, from where sprung people like Bertie Auld. They probably have more nicknames than any other club in Scotland – the Jags, the Harry Wraggs, the Maryhill Magyars, the Old Unpredictables – and their ground is a strange haphazard sort of affair, with an old stand with a sort of internal pavilion in one corner, two new modern stands – one named after their best ever player called Jackie Husband – and then nothing at all at the other end (the end nearest the town!) It is often called Firhill for Thrills. Certainly, most opposition teams would leave there totally aware that they had been in a fight in the old days, but only rarely was there any great consistent challenge to the hegemony of the larger clubs.

They have had two moments of glory. One was away back in 1921, when they won the Scottish Cup thanks in part to Jimmy 'Napoleon' McMenemy, whom Celtic had allowed to leave when he still had some football in him, and the other was the one which sent Jock Stein into paroxysms of rage when they beat Celtic 4–1 in the Scottish League Cup Final of October 1971 – a result that stunned Scotland, but was somehow or other in tune with Partick Thistle's penchant for upsetting the odds big time before relapsing into unremitting mediocrity. 'Ilka doggie has his day,' they say. Maybe, but it was one of Celtic's dark days and cannot be entirely explained away by the absence of Billy McNeill and the injury to Jimmy Johnstone.

Since 1971, Partick had staved off the threat of bankruptcy more than once, and had been one of those teams of whom it was difficult to say in what particular division of the Scottish League they would find themselves at any one time. This year, under an articulate and intelligent character called Alan Archibald, they were at least holding their own. In recent weeks they had played well against Aberdeen and Rangers, but lost narrowly in both cases.

A Friday night in December is not perhaps the ideal time for a football match, but the Celtic fans were there in force (the Thistle fans less so) and they were rewarded with some good goals and a fine 4–1 victory. The weather was cold, but not desperately so for December, and dry, the pitch played well, and there was some good football on show, not least from Thistle in the early stages who held Celtic out until almost half-time.

Celtic's best man that night was Leigh Griffiths. All season there would be a rivalry between Dembele and Griffiths for the goal-scoring job, and Griffiths played tonight as if he had a point to prove. First of all, he crossed from the left for Armstrong to score just before half-time, then he took a free kick for Armstrong to shoot past the goalkeeper, although the ball may have taken a slight deflection on the way. Then came the goal of the game, when he robbed a Thistle defender, spun round and scored – all with his left foot! He clearly made us all sit up and take notice that night! Callum McGregor finished things off near the end.

Before that, however, we'd had the one black mark of the night when Partick were allowed to score from a header with the Celtic defence asleep. It was a makeshift back four of Izaguirre, Sviatchenko, Lustig and Gamboa, and questions would have to be asked about why, from a free-kick, the Thistle man was allowed to rise and score unchallenged. It happened again, but this time with no fatal result. Still, 4–1 was a more than competent performance, we reckoned, as we headed homewards with the horrible thought that there was no football tomorrow, so maybe some Christmas shopping was in order.

But we were back again to Celtic Park on Tuesday night to see Hamilton Accies, who came out wearing a light blue strip instead of the expected red. Hamilton Accies are a team who punch well above their weight in Scottish football, and therefore one has to have a sneaking admiration for them and what they have achieved. Like so many other clubs, they suffer from the geography of simply being too close to Glasgow, but as early as 1911, they took Celtic to a replay in a Scottish Cup Final and have been a constant factor of Scottish football, reaching the Final of the Scottish Cup again in 1935. They earned our love in January 1987 when a man by the name of Adrian Sprott scored the only goal of the game to put Rangers out of the Scottish Cup.

Now managed by a decent-looking chap by the name of Martin Canning, the Accies were holding their own in the Premiership, albeit already looking this season as if they might be candidates for the drop. They had in their ranks an ex-Celtic man by the name of Massimo Donati, an Italian who, in season 2007/08, had played several games for Celtic, including some particularly fine performances against Aberdeen and Shakhtar Donetsk, but who failed to live up to his early promise and had not quite made the grade.

The scoreline of Celtic 1 Hamilton 0 does not sound all that impressive, but it was misleading, for Hamilton played well above themselves, defended well and Celtic had to work hard to get the better of them. The Celtic team selection had Sviatchenko and Simunovich together in the central defence, and they played solidly together apart from the time that Donati was allowed a weak header at

Erik Sviatchenko.

Gordon. Up front Rodgers paired the rivals Dembele and Griffiths together – a rare combination, but the only goal of the game came from a lovely piece of co-operation between the two of them. Dembele had the ball as he was running at goal but noticed that Griffiths was in a better position, so he unselfishly passed the ball to him. Griffiths almost made a pig's ear of it, but did eventually score. This was in the 36th minute.

The second half might have seen a goal feast, but chances were missed, the goalkeeper and the defenders had good games, and the game finished 1–0 with Celtic now 11 points clear at the top of the League. A wry smile may have appeared on a few faces when we heard that we had seen more football tonight than anyone in Aberdeen – for their game against Motherwell had to be abandoned early in the first half when the floodlights failed! The fans at Pittodrie were distinctly unhappy about all this, as we would have been in similar circumstances, but we could at least reckon that we did pay debts. First, we had Rangers not paying their income tax, and now Aberdeen not paying their electric bill...! But Celtic could look the whole world in the eye, and we would meet Hamilton again in eleven days' time at New Douglas Park on Christmas Eve, and this would be a different type of game altogether.

The week before Christmas is traditionally the worst week of the year for attendances. Too many Christmas parties, Christmas shopping expeditions plus the general question of whether it can be afforded, as well as the general considerations of climate and temperature. The crowd at Parkhead to see Dundee on December was given as 37,404. If this was true, it was considerably short of the average home gate this year, and certainly there did look as if there was a lack of bodies.

Those who missed this game missed a lot. Celtic played with a weakened side – Scott Brown was suspended, and one or two others were given a rest. Rodgers came out and said that he did not think that Dembele and Griffiths were a good pair together, and on this occasion it was Griffiths who was given the nod. Ryan Christie, Nir Bitton, Gary Mackay-Steven were all given a start, and although none of these players necessarily let themselves down, the first half saw a distinct lack of zip about Celtic.

Yet they were on top throughout, and on several occasions really should have done a lot better in front of goal. Most of the crowd had decided that it was half-time and had gone to the toilet or to stand in the painfully slow queues for the refreshment stalls when Tommy Rogic was needlessly fouled well outside the penalty area. It seemed too far out, but Leigh Griffiths did not think so, as he hit the ball from about 25 yards to beat the goalkeeper and to put Celtic 1–0 up at half-time.

The atmosphere in the ground changed noticeably after that, and Celtic came out for the second half to a crowd that was far noisier than it had been before the break. Very soon they had further cause to cheer when, after Celtic had peppered the Dundee goal for a while and Dundee were unable to get the ball away, the ball came to Nir Bitton outside the box, who fired through a ruck of players to put Celtic 2–0 up. He seems to like playing at home to Dundee when Celtic are playing to the Jock Stein end. We recalled how at the end of the 2014/15 season in the game that more or less won the League for Celtic, the Israeli had also scored a great goal against Dundee at that end.

And that seemed to be that. We expected more goals, but they did not come and then as the whole ground were singing 'In the Heat of Lisbon' (so it must have been about the 67th minute!), with the lights from the mobile phones on to make the whole ground look like a massive Christmas tree, Dundee pulled one back. From then on there was a certain amount of tension in the air, and indeed towards the end Dundee might have equalised if their forward Faissal El Bakhtaoui, who had made some good ground, had been a better shot. As it happened, he fired it over the bar and Celtic finished their sixteenth League game of the season, still only having dropped these two galling points at lowly Inverness.

And then it was Partick Thistle again in midweek, again before a sparse crowd at Celtic Park, but once again it was a victory. This was the game that should have been played away back in August when Celtic were given permission to postpone it to take part in a pre-season tournament. It all seemed so long ago now! Thistle had, not without cause, resented this permission given to Celtic, and it was unfortunate for them that they had to go to Celtic Park when they were now bottom of the League. Celtic claimed unconvincingly that there were 55,000 there that wet Tuesday midwinter night, but one would have to be very naïve to believe that when one looked at the empty seats. If the crowd for the Dundee game was given as 37,404, tonight's crowd looked no more than that.

You would never have thought, however, that Thistle were bottom of the League. They put up a brave fight, and came close on several occasions. The only

Jozo Simunovich.

goal of the game came when Scott Sinclair was on hand to hit home a free-kick from Liam Henderson on the right. This happened early on in the game, but if we were expecting a goal deluge after that, we were to be sadly disappointed. Celtic always were the better side, as one would have expected, but they were unable to capitalise on their outfield superiority, and the referee's final whistle came as a relief. It was noticeable as well that when the small knot of Partick supporters clapped their team off at the end, quite a few Celtic supporters joined in. This was no great Glasgow solidarity, but rather an indication that Thistle were really too good a team to be relegated, as indeed events in the New Year would prove.

Once again, Brendan Rodgers made changes. Liam Henderson and Callum McGregor were both given starts, and an 18-year-old called Calvin Miller was given a start at left-back. His replacement by the much more experienced Emilio Izaguirre after about an hour was not necessarily a comment on Calvin's performance so much as an illustration of Brendan Rodgers' thinking, in that he felt that the boy should get a chance, but should be introduced gently into the game.

There were certainly a few shortcomings in Celtic's play tonight, but it was another victory, and you cannot ask for much more. We were now at midwinter's day, and there were still another three games to be played before the New Year, as our thoughts were beginning to be dominated by the fixture at Ibrox on New Year's Eve. Fortunately, we did not take our eyes of the ball, for there were another two games as well – Hamilton at New Douglas Park on Christmas Eve, and Ross County at Parkhead on 28 December.

Callum McGregor would not have spent a Merry Christmas. He certainly would not have exchanged very many presents with referee Willie Collum, who sent him off just after half-time for a tackle on a Hamilton man that seemed to be no more than an accidental collision, from which Callum tried to withdraw. Granted, he had already been booked (for something equally innocuous), but this was an outrageous decision from the ever-controversial Willie Collum. Brendan Rodgers exploded in outrage (something that he did very seldom) and the media backed him up. Had Christmas not come immediately afterwards, a great deal more would have been made of it, one feels.

The game itself was almost embarrassingly one-sided, and one got the impression that Celtic would have won the game with only six men, let alone ten. The weather was a bit squally with a few rain showers, the team wore the horrible black strip with the gold trimmings and there could be little doubt that it was a somewhat surreal atmosphere for the crowd given as 5,003. New Douglas Park is a strange stadium. The Celtic end actually affords not a bad view, but at the other end, there is not very much. Sometimes you can see a bus, today there was some kind of a canvas with advertisements, and if you looked hard enough you could see the supermarket on the hill where, as I recall, stood the old Douglas Park. New Douglas Park is also one of two stadia in Scotland (Falkirk being the other) where I have watched a football match from a 'gazebo' as it is pompously put. You and I might be more inclined to use the word 'tent'.

Not everyone likes artificial pitches, but there are times when you just have to play on them. Leigh Griffiths continued his good form of late by scoring a good goal in the first half before he went off with a strain, and then the classy Stuart Armstrong (one of the clear successes of Brendan Rodgers' first half-season) scored a Christmas cracker of a goal with a fierce drive from about 25 yards, and then both substitutes James Forrest and Moussa Dembele combined to score a third, this being Moussa's first goal since the League Cup Final.

This game then petered out, and Celtic won comfortably with the supporters in great voice. Innovative as always and aware of the season of the year, they sang:

Last Christmas I gave you my heart,
The very next day you gave it away!
This Christmas, to save me the pain
I'll give it to Brendan Rodgers!

and other such joyful ditties. They were now 14 points ahead of Rangers.

Santa Claus came and went, the turkey was consumed and a lot of alcohol, one presumes, before the next game, which was when Ross County came to town on Wednesday, 28 December. Once again, the crowd was large, given as 55,000 but clearly a little short of that, and there was a gallant band of Dingwall supporters, something that did them a great deal of credit.

Callum McGregor was unavailable thanks to his contretemps with Mr Collum on Christmas Eve, so a start was given to Ryan Christie. It wasn't so much a question of the jury still being out on this lad as they hadn't really had a great deal of time to study the evidence. He was a good player, but not really able to command a place in the strong Celtic starting line-up, particularly in the midfield. He would go on loan to Aberdeen in the January window. Tonight he had a good game, and there clearly was a place for him at Celtic Park, at least in the long run.

The game started quite brightly with Ross County, having not a bad season so far, determined to show what they could do. They had never ever won at Parkhead (they had at Hampden twice beaten us, as we recalled painfully) and in a game like this, they had little to lose. Teams like Ross County coming to Celtic Park are not really under a great deal of pressure because they have nothing to lose. No one expects them to win, and no one will be sacked by an irate Board of Directors the following day. Some teams decide to 'park the bus' and defend for a draw; others, like Ross County, have a go.

It was indeed quite a good game for the first 45 minutes, but class will out. Scott Sinclair came close with a header but it was Erik Sviatchenko who opened the scoring. The ever-popular Erik had scored a header or two in the past, but this time it was a rather brilliant piece of play where he picked the ball up just inside the County half and advanced, realising that the defence were allowing him to do so. They were concentrating on marking men like Griffiths and Sinclair. Sviatchenko, then still outside the box, fired through the crowded defence and into the left corner with County's goalkeeper slow to 'wise up' to what was going on.

Then, just on half-time, it was Stuart Armstrong who once again scored a fine goal, beating a defender one way, then another before firing in a fine shot. It was a goal that was somehow typical of Celtic in 2016. Gone were the tippy-tappy days of trying to walk the ball into the net that were so frustrating to watch. The players were now not afraid to shoot and they got their due rewards.

The second half was slightly duller but enlivened by the Green Brigade, as normal. It was fairly clear from an early stage that there was not going to be any

Ross County comeback and thus Celtic were now a small matter of 16 points ahead – and with a game in hand! But the main topic of conversation in the stands that night, as interest in the Ross County game began to flag, was the Hogmanay clash.

Given the relative standings of the two clubs in the League table, it was not exactly going to be a League decider, but that did not in any way diminish the interest in the fixture. It would be Celtic's first trip to Ibrox for a very long time – since 2012, in fact – and although one could never say that an Old Firm fixture was even 'comparatively' meaningless for either side, it probably meant more to Rangers than it did to us. They would find it far more difficult to recover from a defeat, for they would be a humiliating 19 points behind – and the season only halfway through! There was also the midwinter break immediately after with some three weeks to brood on what had happened.

The date was controversial, but no more so than in the past when Rangers and Celtic used to play each other on New Year's Day. The lunchtime kick-off was, of course, set by the demands of TV companies, but it did, we were reassured, have the advantage that it would be more difficult for supporters to get tanked up on alcohol before the game started. Not a bit of it! Where there is a will there is a way, and there was quite a great deal of evidence that alcohol had been imbibed in copious quantity before the start of the game. It was, after all, Hogmanay!

Celtic were still without Kieran Tierney, but as they had been well served by Emilio Izaguirre in the meantime, it was hardly a problem. Sviatchenko and Simunovich were the central-defenders and Lustig the other full-back. Up front Dembele was preferred to Griffiths (Moussa loved playing against Rangers, and the hate directed at him on Rangers websites and social media proved how much they feared him) and the midfield was a very strong-looking one of Armstrong, Brown, McGregor and Forrest (all Scottish!) with Sinclair partnering Dembele up front, although one could also argue that Forrest was a forward and Sinclair a midfielder. Please yourself! One of the strengths of this Celtic set-up was its versatility.

On paper, Celtic looked far superior to Rangers, and certainly the press and the bookmakers thought so. On the other hand, the game was at Ibrox, the desperate Rangers management had a support to appease and of course 'desperation' is a great motivator. Rangers supporters had actually surprised quite a lot of Celtic fans, and indeed the Scottish media, by sticking with them through all their crises, and today they were there in strength. One has to give them credit for that, although some of their singing and chanting was far from pleasant. Arrogance was still there, it has to be said. There would be a lot less of that at the end of the game.

Both teams started kicking towards the opposition support, as it were, and the pace was the usual one of hard tackles, fast running and everyone going hammer and tongs. The weather was as typical midwinter Glasgow as one would be likely to get – dark, rainy, although not particularly cold. You could almost sense the tension all over Scotland as the nation settled down to watch the game – tension, that is, in the pubs, clubs and bars (and indeed private houses) where things could get distinctly noisy. Even for neutrals, it was actually not a bad way of spending Hogmanay.

It was Rangers who opened the scoring. Tavernier made ground down the right and crossed for Kenny Miller to score. Ah, Kenny Miller. He seems to have been around for about thirty years – but his best Old Firm goal was for Celtic! Fittingly and ironically, Garner was on the ground injured when Rangers scored. Was this telling Rangers something?

That was in the first quarter of an hour, and it meant that Celtic had loads of time to fight back. Gradually, the midfield took a grip, the ball began to be passed around, we hit the post at one point and brought out several good saves from Wes Foderingham. But it was Moussa Dembele who fired us level when he was left in space at a corner kick from Scott Sinclair as the Rangers defence made the mistake of 'pushing and shoving' rather than watching the ball. Dembele was able to control the ball and score his fifth goal against Rangers since his arrival.

That was the score at half-time, but the odds were now definitely swinging to Celtic if they hadn't been before. Those of us with a little goodness in our heart and with no desire to spoil anyone's New Year might have settled for a draw (after all, 16 points ahead is enough, is it not?) but Celtic were ruthless and relentless. Dembele fluffed his lines in front of goal with a dreadful miskick, then a downward header of his bounced up and hit the bar before Sinclair hit the side net from the rebound.

It was Sinclair who got the winner. Patrick Roberts, who had come on for James Forrest, released Stuart Armstrong down the right, and crossed for Scott Sinclair to score and to create delirium behind that goal. Twenty minutes remained, and during that time both teams came close with Celtic having the balance of the play, although it would have to be admitted that Rangers did have hard luck as they hit the post. But then again, Celtic had hit the same post in the first half, and when referee Steven McLean (much despised and pilloried in the past for his howler of a game in the Scottish Cup semi-final of 2015 against Inverness, but who had a good game today) blew for full time, there was little doubt that Celtic were the better team.

And so the New Year bells saw Celtic 19 points clear and a game in hand. That spoke for itself. 2016 had been a good one. The six months of Brendan Rodgers had taken Celtic to new planes of achievement, and the crowd of Celtic moaners (those who secretly rather enjoy the team doing badly so that they can pontificate) had to shut up. We were on to something really good, we felt, and Happy New Year for 2017 really meant it! Rangers and Aberdeen fans whom we met over the New Year period had that quiet, chastened, resigned look about them as they wished us a Happy New Year. They knew how good Celtic were, even though it hurt to admit it. And how sweet was the sound of silence!

CHAPTER **TEN**
RESUMPTION

It would not be easy to find many Scottish football fans having a good word to say about the winter shutdown. One can understand why the players like a break, although one's sympathies tend to evaporate when one hears of them going off to sunnier climes when they could be entertaining their fans at home. But fans, as Jock Stein kept saying, are the lifeblood of the game. 'Football, without fans, is nothing.' But, for a couple of weeks in January, there is nothing for them to see!

One suspects, once again, the malign influence of David Murray here, for the idea gained currency, impressing the gullible in the media, round about the turn of the century along with some other crackers of ideas like games kicking off at 6.05 p.m. on a Sunday night, the Scottish Premier League being a different entity from the Scottish Football, and Inverness Caledonian Thistle playing their home games in Aberdeen! No kidding, you youngsters, that was what happened! And all in the name of making Scottish football a lot better! It succeeded too, didn't it? Oh my goodness, it did! All these bankruptcies! Especially the famous one! And the sustained and repeated successes in Europe!

The problem with a midwinter shutdown in Scotland is that the month of January (and indeed every other month) is so unpredictable. Central Europe is a different matter, for snow can be relied upon to fall there, and it makes sense to close down for a spell. But statistically in Scotland the worst month of the year is February, and there have been times when December has not been great either. It would be annoying (but it would also serve them right!) if the winter shutdown weeks coincided with a mild spell, and the bad weather descended in February!

But perhaps the greenhouse effect (if you believe in that) has changed it all anyway. It does give the more geekish Celtic fans (by which I mean people like me, who like watching football in any shape or form) an opportunity to go to a game in a division other than the Premier League, or even to go to a game in England. (Other divisions, apart from the Scottish Premiership, seem to be made of sterner stuff!) Other than that, I find it very difficult to say anything in favour of a winter shutdown.

There was always, of course, the 'transfer window' which 'slammed shut' at the end of January, or as someone put it, 'TV for the gullible'. Every year all sorts of naïve stuff appears in the press, and in particular on Sky Sports, about huge 'marquee' signings, and in Scotland we have journalists and pundits making a fool of themselves by assuring us that someone was about to sign for Celtic, Rangers, Aberdeen or whoever. Eoin Jess of Aberdeen, for example, was almost over the threshold at Ibrox year after year! Forgive us for laughing when it all didn't happen!

Journalists, of course, have to fill pages, and these wicked agents – the curse of the modern game – are always potentially on the make, so speculation is fuelled, but I at least am always quite glad to see 1 February and no damage done. We recall bitterly how Tony Mowbray came to spectacular grief in January 2010 by trying to almost rebuild the team. It all came about as a gut reaction to one awful Sunday at Tannadice in November 2009, when the central defence of Steve McManus and Gary Caldwell lost two awful late goals from corner kicks. The baby then had to be thrown out with the bathwater in January. You simply cannot do it, and in any case, sober analysis would tell one that the best players are not always available in January, and if they are, why? Why is a club keen to sell a player halfway through a season? The answer is amazingly obvious.

Celtic's first game back was in the Scottish Cup (and how delighted we were to see Kieran Tierney back wearing the hoops) and there were two other games in January, both at Celtic Park. One was a rearranged game against St Johnstone on Burns Night, 25 January, and the other was the visit of Hearts on Sunday, 29 January.

St Johnstone have a tendency to do well at Celtic Park, winning there on several occasions, and always being hard to break down. I have often felt that with better support from the city of Perth, they could be a real force in Scottish football, and in early 2017 they certainly had a good Manager in Tommy Wright. Their policy in coming to Celtic Park that night was to defend certainly, but also be prepared to attack on the break where necessary. They seemed to be denied a clear penalty late in the game, and they came very close to earning at least a draw.

Two landmarks were reached tonight. One was Scott Brown's 400th appearance for the club – and it was very much in the mould of his previous 399 – tough, hard-working, aggressive, combining the old Roy Aitken combative mode of play but without Roy's carelessness and propensity to give the ball away. The other landmark was that the team now equalled the record set by Jock Stein's team in the late 1960s of twenty-six domestic games without defeat (Willie Maley's team in the Great War had done better than that, but 1916/17 was a season with strange circumstances), so the team was clearly in good company, even though it would have to be conceded that the opposition in Stein's era was considerably better with Rangers, Aberdeen, Dunfermline, Kilmarnock, Hibs and Dundee United all having strong sides.

Before a large crowd of over 50,000 enthusiastic fans, who were possibly delivering their own verdict on what they thought of the winter shutdown, St Johnstone possibly had the better of the first half, hitting the post on one occasion, although Celtic had their chances as well. Scott Sinclair, now instantly recognisable because of his multi-coloured hairstyle (another bad effect of the winter shutdown!) was off form, as indeed was Dembele showing signs of rustiness, and the teams turned round with the game still goalless.

The game changed in the second half, with Celtic putting a little more pressure on the Perth defence, but there was still a disturbing lack of penetration. The 67th minute with the impressive commemoration of Lisbon came and went, and we were beginning to think that we were not going to get a goal. But we did, and it was from an unlikely source.

Dedryck Boyata was in danger of becoming the 'forgotten man' of Celtic Park. He had only played once in competitive games since the start of the season under Brendan Rodgers, and in so far as anyone talked about the big Belgian at all, it was in the context of him having been a 'Deila' man, and he would probably get punted

Dedryck Boyata.

for a minimal price anonymously to someone like Crystal Palace or Norwich City in the summer. He was big and powerful certainly, but a little clumsy on the ball on occasion, and as long as Celtic had the adequate central defence of Simunovich and Sviatchenko with Lustig able to cover if necessary, there did not seem to be any great need for him.

But he had reappeared against Albion Rovers at Airdrie on Saturday and tonight he had been impressive in defence until the 72nd minute, when he earned his place, more or less, for the rest of the season, with a bullet header home of a Stuart Armstrong corner. It was a fine goal and much appreciated by the fans and his teammates, and it did give us a hint of something that at the moment the team, for all its admirable qualities in other respects, did not have – namely, an aerial presence.

St Johnstone kept working hard, but referee Andrew Dallas brought the game to an end and we departed relieved rather than triumphant – and 22 points ahead of Rangers and 24 ahead of Aberdeen. Mind you, the pedants pointed out, Aberdeen had a game in hand! We now had Hearts on Sunday at Parkhead, followed by Aberdeen at home as well, and then we were back to St Johnstone, this time at Perth.

So it was Hearts to finish off the truncated month of January. Hearts are a hard team to like, and some of their supporters are even more so, particularly those with a very large chip on their shoulder about Celtic. Yet there are some decent people among them as well, particularly the older ones who recall Willie Bauld, Dave Mackay and Alec Young with a wistful tear in their eye, particularly when they compare them with today.

The management of Hearts over the past half century has not always been what it could or should be. In fact, there are times when it has defied belief and bordered on the idiotic. They once, for example, sacked their Manager George Burley (at a time when they were going well!) on a Saturday morning a couple of hours before kick-off (no kidding) and this year, following the departure of Robbie Neilson to England, they appointed, apparently on the advice of BBC Radio Scotland, a chap called Ian Cathro who had by all accounts been a good coach and indeed Assistant Manager of Newcastle United but whose credentials for managing a Scottish Premier League team were limited. Stories soon started to leak about influence from others behind the scenes, and it seemed to most people that Cathro was merely a front man for all that was going so horribly wrong at Tynecastle. And yet, in the early part of the season, they had been mentioned as potential title challengers.

Hearts supporters were entitled to feel bewildered, for there seemed to be a new team on the park nearly every week, and although there was some talent around, the performances of the team (two wins out of the last seven) was considered to be unacceptable by the support. They had required a replay to get past Raith Rovers in the Scottish Cup, and this sunny (if still a little cold) Sunday saw a fairly small Hearts contingent in the away corner. Time was when Hearts would produce a big support to hurl abuse and hate at us; now even their 'bawheids' seemed to be giving up!

The Celtic crowd, however, were upbeat as they watched their team beat the record which they had equalled on Wednesday. Neither member of the strike force, Griffiths or Dembele, was playing as both had picked up injuries, but that hardly mattered as Celtic romped to a 4–0 victory over dispirited opponents who seemed to have given up and accepted the inevitable long before Celtic's late flurry of goals made the scoreline reflect the balance of play.

It was the excellent Callum McGregor who put Celtic ahead in the first half, making a capital job of finishing a Scott Sinclair through ball. Hearts did compel their former goalkeeper Craig Gordon to make a good save, but it was mainly Celtic, although frustratingly and worryingly, they could not finish things off, until in the 77th minute, Kieran Tierney crossed for Scott Sinclair to slide in and score. Soon after that, the game was definitely all over when Tierney again, this time in conjunction with Liam Henderson, set up Patrick Roberts to drive in to the roof of the net. Then just on the final whistle, Scott Sinclair scored from the penalty spot after young Jack Aitchison, brought on as a substitute, had been brought down.

The victory was comprehensive and welcome. What this game did show was the sheer depth of squad that Celtic had. Tonight, the loss of the strike force (both of them) would have floored lesser outfits, but the absence was hardly noticed. What was remarkable was the sheer amount of excellent players like Cristian Gamboa, Erik Sviatchenko, Tommy Rogic, Emilio Izaguirre, Callum McGregor, Liam Henderson, Gary Mackay-Steven, Ryan Christie and others who simply could not be guaranteed a place in this Celtic starting XI when they could have walked into any other team in Scotland, and many in England. Ryan Christie, in fact, went to Aberdeen on loan before the end of January. We wondered about this, and a few expressed reservations, but sober reflection saw that it was for the best, certainly for Ryan. With Aberdeen, he would get first XI experience and would surely come back a better player.

Normally in such circumstances of a large squad of players, some of whom could become distinctly unsatisfied and unfulfilled, there can be a certain amount of friction and the occasional 'falling out'. This did not seem to be happening, or at least we never got to hear about it if it did. The gutter press did now and again on dull days try to make something happen on this front, but they never succeeded. Celtic were a cohesive unit, and a highly successful one as well, and as January now gave way to February, the team seemed to be getting better as the days lengthened.

CHAPTER **ELEVEN**
CONSOLIDATION

Aberdeen were next to appear at Celtic Park on 1 February in Celtic's three-in-a-
row run of home games. Anyone who felt that this game had any sort of bearing
on the destination of the Championship needed a reality check, and the contrast
between now and a year ago was quite stark. Last year in the same week, the two
teams met at Pittodrie and Aberdeen won, thereby triggering a bout of speculation
that there was now a challenge. That could not have been said this year. Even a
substantial win for Aberdeen would only have had some psychological value for
the rest of the season, particularly the Scottish Cup. We were already counting
down the games before we could say we were champions. It would have had to
be a monumental crash before anyone could even contemplate now losing the
League.

None of this, however, in any way lessened the determination of Aberdeen to
break the seemingly unbreakable stranglehold that Celtic exercised over them.
Celtic had already beaten them this season at Parkhead, Pittodrie and, of course,
Hampden in the Scottish League Cup Final. Tonight, however, they must have
felt that they had a chance, for Celtic were still without both Leigh Griffiths and
Moussa Dembele, and also Stuart Armstrong, a man who had come on by leaps
and bounds this season. The Dons on the other hand were at full strength, and had
restarted well from the midwinter break, beating Dundee, a team who had given
them grief in the past, 3–0 last Friday night. Considering the distance involved, a
goodly number of their supporters attended that night.

The night was cold but dry on Wednesday, 1 February, and the first half was an
intriguing affair with neither side asserting any dominance, the round of applause
that Aberdeen got from their supporters as they left the field telling its own story.
Last week against St Johnstone it was Dedryck Boyata who broke the deadlock,
and it was the same man who did it this week. This time it was a free kick from
Scott Sinclair on the left, but the header was just as good and just as accurate.

From now on, Celtic took control and remained in command. There was no further scoring, but one had the impression that even if Aberdeen had got back into the game, Celtic would have been able to move up a gear. Aberdeen were unable to get the best out of their talismanic Jonny Hayes, and there was a resigned look of acceptance on their faces at the end.

The main effect of this game was psychological. We all knew, whether we supported Aberdeen, Celtic or anyone else who the champions were going to be. It was interesting, however, to try to pretend to be an Aberdeen supporter, and there were areas with which one could identify. Those of us who were around in the 1990s and the 1960s will recall going into games against Rangers expecting to be beaten, feeling that they there was a divine right and arrogance emanating from Ibrox saying that it was preordained that they would win, while at Parkhead there was a lack of mental toughness to counteract all that. This was the way that Aberdeen felt about us at this moment in time, and it would have its effect on the players, some of whom were giving indications already that they were wanting to leave at the end of the season.

But for Celtic, they did not seem able to do any wrong, and now we were off to St Johnstone at McDiarmid Park on Sunday, 5 February. St Johnstone, of course, were the last Scottish team to beat Celtic – in an irrelevant League game at the end of last season when the League was well won – and the tussle between the two of them in August had been a good one. Not only that, but when the teams had met less than a fortnight ago at Celtic Park, the Saints had put up a strong resistance before conceding to Boyata's header. They were having a good season and would be good enough to qualify for Europe, a tremendous achievement for a city with fewer footballing ambitions and aspirations than most.

This was obvious yet again when we looked at the St Johnstone support, pitifully outnumbered by the travelling Celts, and we wondered yet again why clubs could be so stupid as to deny themselves money. We had the phenomenon of hundreds (and I mean hundreds) of Celtic fans standing with money in hand wanting to buy a ticket to get in, in some cases promising faithfully to remove colours and behave themselves among the St Johnstone supporters, but being told to move on. They went to the pub and spent their money on drink while watching the game on TV. And all the time, there were rows and rows of empty seats. Why do provincial clubs insist on denying themselves money like this? All that is required is a thoughtful readjustment of seating arrangements for the days that Celtic arrive. I cannot believe that it is difficult, and the financial gains would be significant.

Be that as it may, the fans at the ground and in the pub saw a very good game, which Celtic won well, even though they were behind for a spell, and needed the benefit of a dodgy penalty to get back into the game. Come to think of it, the penalty wasn't so much 'dodgy' as sheer wrong and Craig Thomson would surely admit this was the case when he saw it on TV afterwards, even though 'seeing it on TV' would give him a huge advantage. Arguments about the penalty tended, however, to overshadow the undeniable fact that this was another great Celtic performance and that Celtic would have won anyway.

It was a dull, raw, Scottish winter day, but the pitch was in good condition and the game was highly entertaining. Celtic gave a start to Liam Henderson and Gary Mackay-Steven, and it was Liam Henderson who scored first, sweeping the ball in from the edge of the box after some good work involving Roberts and Brown. Liam then did a fairly passable impersonation of Robin Hood to celebrate the goal. But then Celtic suffered two blows when first Keith Watson headed in a goal after simply out-muscling and out-jumping the Celtic defence. Before half-time Saints were in the lead, and Dedryck Boyata, who had scored two good goals of late with his head, scored a third, but this time it was an own goal when he was unable to divert the ball past the post, and then beat Craig Gordon instead. It was a very unfortunate occurrence.

At half-time we were all agreed on two things. One was that St Johnstone had indeed done well and maybe even deserved to be ahead; the other was that the Perth men had better enjoy their brief moment of supremacy, for Celtic would fight back. And how! They roared into attack and, although it was unfortunate that they got that penalty the way that they did, they would have overwhelmed Saints sooner or later. Kieran Tierney did well on the left, beating a man and then firing into the penalty area. The Saints man, only a few yards away, turned, the ball hit his hip and the referee, thinking he had used an arm, gave a penalty. He really should have consulted, and there really is a strong case for the use of TV evidence in these circumstances.

It did prove, too, that Celtic get the benefit of refereeing errors as well. One does get a little fed up now and again of those among our support who think that referees are all in the pay of Ibrox, that they roll up their trouser legs now and again and shake hands in funny ways before going home to practise their flute-playing for July. That there has been an element of this in the past is undeniable, and yes, we have had a few raw deals in the past – a couple of Hampden semi-finals spring to mind – but sometimes we get the benefit as well. In any case, any referee bribed by Rangers in the past few years would not have earned very much! On the other hand, if they were paying referees in the more distant past, that is maybe why they went bust!

Dembele had only recently come on for Gary Mackay-Steven, and he slotted home effortlessly. It was he who put Celtic ahead with another fine drive through a ruck of players after some excellent build-up work. Scott Sinclair made it four after being released by the excellent Patrick Roberts, and the fifth goal involving Mikael Lustig's rabona and the ball being passed effortlessly to Dembele after virtually every Celtic player had been involved, was simply a thing of class.

It meant that St Johnstone could not complain too much about the wrong penalty decision, because Celtic finished well on top, giving TV audiences in Scotland and throughout the world clear and ample evidence of how good they were. McDiarmid Park is to be commended on the speed with which it allows fans to depart, in contrast to some other grounds (guess who!) who have occasionally seemed to take a sadistic delight in keeping buses waiting, and it was a happy bunch of Celtic fans who departed Perth that afternoon. Some of us didn't even know how many points we were ahead. It didn't seem to matter.

The St Johnstone game had combined success with entertainment value, and that surely had to be what Celtic was all about, as Celtic luminaries like Bertie Auld and the late Jock Stein kept saying. There was, however, one fly in the ointment as February progressed and the European tournaments began to return to the TV screen once again, and that was that there was no Celtic on the European stage. It remained very easy for people outwith Scotland to talk dismissively of a 'one horse race' – indeed it was virtually impossible to disagree with them – and it remained annoying and vexatious that we did not have another chance to show how we could compete at a higher level. Manchester City and their fans at least had a certain respect for Celtic. What a pity that we hadn't done better and qualified in the autumn! Some of the European football on TV that February was rather poor, and we felt, with justice, that we could have done better.

But it was a learning experience. We were a 'job in progress' in European terms. The rate of progress was quite phenomenal. We were growing and growing. The support was mobilised, and we were expecting great things both for the remainder of this season and for the immediate future under the tutelage of Brendan Rodgers, who had come home to 'lead the green and white'. It was my privilege at about this time to take a party of children to Lennoxtown to see the facilities and meet some of the players. Scott Sinclair 'oh so wonderful!' was – irrespective of his horrendous hairstyle, which was 'oh so frightening' – a humble man from Bath who had grown up supporting Manchester United but who now loved Celtic. Kieran Tierney was a quiet-spoken, shy boy, possibly even unaware of his huge talent, and Brendan Rodgers was a very small man, in contrast to his huge stature in the eyes of the support. But they were all, just as they used to say about Jimmy Quinn, 'just like an ordinary man'.

The next game was the Scottish Cup tie against Inverness Caledonian Thistle on 12 February, and after that there were another couple of home games against Lanarkshire opposition Motherwell and Hamilton Academical, both of which were solid performances won 2–0 as Celtic continued their inexorable progress towards the League title.

Singing and dancing after the League is won at Tynecastle.

Scott Brown and Craig Gordon lift the Scottish Cup for Celtic's 37th time.

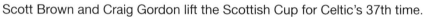

Scott Brown lifts the League trophy.

Brendan Rodgers with the Scottish Cup.

The greatest show on earth!

Larsson, McGrory, Stein, Walfrid, Maley, Johnstone and Burns – all honorary members of the Green Brigade.

Efe Ambrose – not perhaps the best football player the world has ever seen, but what a backflip!

Everything there apart from Mikael Lustig's jacket!

Grim determination before the start of the Scottish Cup Final.

Brendan Rodgers picks up the Scottish Cup.

Patrick Roberts shoots for goal in a game against Hearts.

Dedryck Boyata and Scott Brown in the thick of it in the Scottish Cup Final.

Happy Celts! Scott Sinclair has just scored a penalty in the Scottish Cup semi-final against Rangers.

Stuart Armstrong has just scored against Rangers and is about to be congratulated by Nir Bitton, James Forrest and Scott Brown. The lads at the back don't seem to be so happy, though!

Referee Bobby Madden and Brendan Rodgers look at each other in what seems to be mutual suspicion!

Scott Brown and Craig Gordon show their delight as Scott lifts the famous three-handled Scottish League Cup.

The first of the season. Celtic show off the first of the treble, the Scottish League Cup, won at the end of November 2016 with a convincing 3–0 victory over Aberdeen.

The Motherwell side which appeared at Celtic Park on 18 February hotched with ex-Celts, not least Manager Mark McGhee who had just thrown a 'hissy fit' after he had been sent to the stand in a 7–2 pumping at Pittodrie. It made for good YouTube viewing, but today he was on his best behaviour. The three ex-Celts in the Motherwell side were Stephen McManus, Scott McDonald and Stephen Pearson, and we wondered how they all would have fared in Brendan Rodgers' side.

McManus had been a reasonable centre-half for us, but had never survived an awful day at Tannadice in November 2009 when, with Celtic winning, Dundee United had scored two goals from corner kicks in the last five minutes. He and Gary Caldwell departed in the following January window. Scott McDonald, who had broken our hearts on that awful day called Black Sunday in May 2005 when with Motherwell before, had had his moments with Celtic, but had always shown a distinct reluctance to shoot from the edge of the box (a definite feature of the current Celtic side was that they were always prepared to do just that) while Stephen Pearson had not been given a long enough run in the team to prove his value.

McManus did not last long that day, disappearing after about five minutes with what looked like a groin strain, and being replaced by a gentleman with the unlikely name of Zak Jules. The game was dour, mirroring the weather, and it was once again a question of when Celtic would break down the stubborn Motherwell defence. It was the said Zak Jules who conceded a penalty to allow Moussa Dembele to score, and then we had a really great vignette from the sometimes-underrated James Forrest, who ran across the Motherwell defence to score a grand individual goal. All this after Liam Henderson had missed an easy chance, and then in the second half, Scott Sinclair put one over the bar when it looked easier to score, after more fine work from Forrest.

This was now Celtic's twentieth domestic win in a row, but we would have to admit that if Leagues were won by hairstyles, Celtic would be in danger of relegation. We have already mentioned the coiffure of Scott Sinclair, but today Moussa Dembele was a similar colour (actually, almost er, orange, which was maybe not the favourite colour down Parkhead way!) and Nir Bitton was now albino. Did no one fancy trying a green and white hairdo?

Celtic made it twenty-one in a row with more or less a carbon copy the following week against Hamilton. This time it was Dembele who scored the two goals in the 2–0 victory. His first was a lovely piece of work on the stroke of half-time as he beat Massimo Donati, then ran in and scored, the other was a penalty kick when the same Massimo Donati brought down Keiran Tierney in the second half. Dembele was then substituted by Leigh Griffiths whose reappearance brought a great cheer from the Celtic crowd. Hamilton put up a reasonable performance, well-organised and disciplined, and had a certain amount of pressure themselves, notably just at the end of the game when they brought a good save out of Craig Gordon. Against that, Celtic missed some easy chances, but it was yet again another regulation win

Thus ended the month of February and we now moved on to the month of March, beginning with the long trip up the A9 to Inverness to meet again the team that were still the only ones who had taken points off us. It would be fair to say that Inverness's late equaliser that day was the highlight of their season so far, for they had not impressed anyone in any other game, certainly not in their recent Scottish Cup trip to Parkhead where they had been on the wrong end of a 6–0 doing.

There were a few signs of early spring as we made our way up the A9. As yet there was no great warmth, or even dryness, but there was daylight until about 6.00 p.m. Frankly, Celtic outclassed the Highlanders on this occasion and there was one moment of what can only be called comedy and it belonged entirely to Stuart Armstrong. There was also a moment of farce as well.

Celtic were 1–0 up at half-time. It had been a bit of a struggle but Scott Sinclair's goal was a joy to behold. He picked up the ball well outside the box, was clearly fouled but the referee played advantage and Scott shot home from a distance. Yet again a shot from outside the box which was a feature of our play this year!

And then came the farcical moment, just a few seconds after the start of the second half. Goalkeeper Fon Williams hideously miskicked an attempted clearance, the ball ballooned up in the air, and Moussa Dembele got the ball, controlled it and coolly placed the ball into the net. But then came the moment when even some of the Inverness supporters had to laugh, as Celtic went three ahead. Celtic had been awarded a free kick on the left side, and possibly just a little far out for a shot, or so we thought. The defence and attackers lined themselves up, and as is the modern custom, the statutory arm-wrestling and manhandling began.

Referee Andrew Dallas stopped everything and took a good minute or so to sort it out, giving stern warnings, threatening yellow cards and penalty kicks and/ or free kicks up the field if there was to be any more of such nonsense. Meanwhile, Stuart Armstrong stood by the ball and waited. Eventually the referee signalled for the kick to be taken, and Stuart calmly smashed the ball home, then turned as if to say that the only thing that really mattered was the ball, and it was in the back of the net! I for one have never understood all this blocking and badgering at set pieces – for it must distract attention from the only important thing, namely this piece of leather! This was an excellent example, and I remain grateful to Stuart Armstrong for showing everyone how to do it!

Late in the game Celtic picked up another goal, when Dembele latched on to a long ball from the excellent Kieran Tierney and placed the ball past Williams. It was a fine 4–0 win, and those of us who had watched the last few games trying to spot the relegation team, wondered whether the dispirited and poorly supported Inverness were to be the team for the drop. It was difficult to find anything good to say about them on this performance. Celtic, however, were just going from strength to strength.

The weekend after the trip to Inverness was taken up with the Scottish Cup game against St Mirren, but the week after that was the visit of Rangers to Celtic Park for the second time that season. It would have been nice if we had been able to win the League at the Rangers game on 12 March, but that was not possible and the earliest we could have realistically hoped for was 19 March at Dens Park. Nevertheless, a game against Rangers still had its own atmosphere, and a great deal was still at stake.

Not only good footballers, but they can count as well! 3 + 3 = 6 (League Titles in a row).

Rangers were in a bit of disarray. They had sacked their Manager Mark Warburton – an honest Englishman, who we always felt could have made a success of a club in a less crazy environment – and they had appointed a Portuguese gentleman by the name of Pedro Caixinha the day before the game. It would be fair to say that no one, unless an avid reader of geekish foreign football websites, had heard of him. He turned up to see the game at Celtic Park, although the team was still being run by caretaker boss Graeme Murty, another fellow who was less than a household name in Glasgow or anywhere else.

The game had a lunchtime kick-off on a pleasant spring day in Glasgow, but although everyone was 'up for it' as one would have expected of an Old Firm match, it was also clear that Celtic quite simply had the better players, and it was no surprise when they scored what was now beginning to look like a trademark Celtic goal from Stuart Armstrong at the edge of the box after he had been fed by James Forrest. Once more we saw the value of Brendan Rodgers encouraging his players to shoot from a distance. Previous Celtic teams had been guilty of trying to walk the ball into the net, or pumping a high ball into the penalty area and hoping for the best.

Rangers fought back in the second half and prevented Celtic from adding to their lead, although once or twice Celtic felt that they had the rough edge of referee Bobby Madden's decisions. The game was heading towards its conclusion when Rangers got their equaliser. Craig Gordon could only parry a fierce drive, and Clint Hill – in the highlight of his hitherto somewhat underperforming career – tapped the ball into the net. There was no further scoring and the game finished 1–1.

One has to stress that the result was 1–1 because the impression given by the media was somewhat different. The impression given was that Rangers had won the European Cup or something. The word 'overdrive' did not quite cover it, as radio, television and newspapers all combined to tell us how good Rangers were. The Scottish media always hoists its true colours when Rangers have a success. Clearly there had been little success to boast about for many years, so there was clearly a need to manufacture some joy. 'Great fightback', 'real character', 'Pedro Caixinha would have been impressed', 'Ibrox spirit' and other vacuous and inane clichés found their way into the national press for the benefit of the gullible... but the score was 1–1!

In fact, Rangers had denied Celtic their twenty-third win in a row! And Celtic were still undefeated! And we were 33 points ahead! Rangers' one point meant that they were not even close to Aberdeen, let alone Celtic! The propaganda barrage continued for several days, while we went about our normal business, recalling the words of Robert Burns perhaps that 'the man o independent mind, he looks and laugh at a' that'. Rangers, we now knew, had to play Celtic twice more before the end of the season. They would now be all fired up, convinced that they were bound to win. Those of us with long memories recalled 1969, when the press convinced everyone with the slightest connection to Ibrox that they were going to beat Celtic in the Scottish Cup Final. The result was Celtic 4 Rangers 0.

Ignoring how good Rangers were in getting a gallant draw against the odds, we now faced the next game. In theory, we could actually win the League at Dens Park, Dundee on Sunday, 19 March, we reckoned. Unfortunately, the day before, Aberdeen beat Hearts 2–0, so this was no longer possible as another six points were still required. Meanwhile the revived, triumphant Rangers beat Hamilton 4–0. They were really beginning to scare us now!

And so it was back up to Bonnie Dundee to take another step towards the title. It was a fine spring day and once again the home team must have been disappointed at the turnout of its own fans. Possibly not, though, for they were well compensated by the TV money. The game was important for Celtic but it was crucial for Dundee, for Paul Hartley's side were now very definitely embroiled in a relegation battle, the development of which, to a neutral at least, was a great deal more exciting than that of the Premiership title which had been a foregone conclusion for so long.

In recent weeks there had been a hint of an indication that Hamilton and Inverness would be the two teams that would go down, but everyone was aware that there were still a lot of games still to go, and of course, in the relegation zone everyone played each other after the 'split'. Playing with the desperation of those fighting for their Premier League survival, the Dee started strongly and might have gone ahead, but slowly Celtic's midfield of McGregor, Armstrong and Brown took charge and it was no real surprise when Celtic took the lead before half-time. It was an ugly, unsatisfactory sort of goal, however, for Jozo Simunovich, off balance, did not seem to get enough on a Forrest cross, but it hit a Dundee defender before going in. This had followed a sustained period of Celtic pressure in which a Boyata header had been cleared off the line, so Celtic's lead was not undeserved.

No criticism, however, is possible about the second goal. It was a sublime header by Stuart Armstrong (he doesn't score a lot with his head) from a cross by the excellent James Forrest. And that seemed to be that, but Dundee kept fighting and in the 76th minute a gentleman by the name of Faissal El Bakhtaoui showed a bit of class when he beat Boyata on the halfway line and ran at the Celtic defence to score. This did at least make the last 15 minutes more interesting than might have been the case, but Celtic rode it out and the game finished 3–1, with Celtic now just needing three points on 2 April against Hearts at Tynecastle to be absolutely certain, although Dundee could do the job for them on 31 March if they beat Aberdeen.

All this was a fortnight away, because there was now an International break. Normally International breaks are irritating distractions, mainly because we in Scotland do not very often have a team to get excited about, but this time, against Slovenia at Hampden, Scotland with Gordon, Tierney, Brown, Armstrong, Forrest and Griffiths on board managed a win with a late winner scored by Chris Martin to keep alive Scotland's fairly slim chances of qualification for the 2018 World Cup in Russia.

It was, however, still an irritating distraction with Celtic so close to the title. But the following week, all Celtic eyes turned to Tynecastle to see if we could win our sixth title in a row, something that would put us on the same level as Willie Maley's side from 1905–10 and would take us two-thirds of the way towards Jock Stein's nine in a row from 1966–74. It was distinguished company. It would also be nice to win the title at Tynecastle in front of that bitter support who took a particular dislike to you when you mentioned a fellow who used to play for Dundee called Albert Kidd.

CHAPTER TWELVE
THE 48th LEAGUE TITLE

Quite a few Celtic fans, one imagines, would have put on the television on the night of Friday, 31 March to see if Celtic could win the League. This would happen if Dundee could beat Aberdeen, and as the game was at Dens Park, where Dundee had put up a fight against Celtic the previous Sunday, there was at least a chance, we felt. Not a bit of it. In what the BBC website describes with devastating candour as 'a horrible night' for Dundee and Paul Hartley, they collapsed totally to a strong and determined Aberdeen side, although no one could have predicted that the hat-trick hero in the 7–0 hammering would be no less a person than defender Andrew Considine. Following such a thrashing from a team that Dundee often considered to be their natural rivals and equals, Manager Paul Hartley would not last long. A doing like that in front of one's home fans cannot be tolerated, and indeed often hints at a little lack of motivation from the players.

And so it was to Tynecastle for the chance to win the Scottish League and to make 2017 join the gallant band of 1893, 1894, 1896, 1898, 1905, 1906, 1907, 1908, 1909, 1910, 1914, 1915, 1916, 1917, 1919, 1922, 1926, 1936, 1938, 1954, 1966, 1967, 1968, 1969, 1970, 1971, 1972, 1973, 1974, 1977, 1979, 1981, 1982, 1986, 1988, 1998, 2001, 2002, 2004, 2006, 2007, 2008, 2012, 2013, 2014, 2015 and 2016 and make it forty-eight Scottish League title wins.

It was, of course, one of these years – 1986 – which remained an open sore with Hearts fans, with Albert Kidd never likely to become the darling of Gorgie Road. The reasons for the sometimes quite irrational hatred of Celtic by Hearts fans had been discussed elsewhere, but it is a shame that the behaviour and demeanour of Hearts fans has sometimes overshadowed the very fine contribution over the years that Hearts have made to Scottish football – one thinks of Bobby Walker of the 1900s, who was reckoned to be almost as good as Jimmy 'Napoleon' McMenemy (and that is saying something!), Tommy Walker (who scored a famous penalty for Scotland at Wembley), Alec Massie, Willie Bauld, Alec Young and Dave MacKay and many others.

But times change, and Hearts, although they have won the Scottish Cup three times in the last twenty years, continue to disappoint their supporters with bizarre and crazy decisions taken at boardroom level. If we think that the Celtic board have done a few mad things in the past and have been out of touch with the supporters, try looking at some of the things that Hearts have done!

But it was a fine day in Edinburgh as Celtic supporters travelled to the capital to find yet again a tiny piece of the north stand allocated to them when, frankly, we could have filled the ground. Admittedly, the phenomenon of empty home supporters' seats was not quite so marked or as blatant as it had been at other grounds, but it was still there. It would be the last chance we would have to see the old main stand, which was to be demolished and replaced by a newer one. The Tynecastle main stand was quaint, built in 1914, but old and sometimes, one felt, quite dangerous with some of the narrow exits with notices painted on the walls telling people to 'Beware of Pickpockets'. That particular notice had been there for some time! It would be sad to see the old stand go, for it had seen some football in its time!

The game slavishly adopted the pattern of so many Celtic games that season. Early pressure from the opposition in which Celtic, with a little luck, survived through a goalkeeper's save or a narrow miss, but then Celtic scored, asserted control and the opposition collapsed. It was Scott Sinclair from the left who gave Celtic the lead with a lovely one-two with Patrick Roberts before crashing the ball into the roof of the net. Scarcely had the acclaim for this wonderful goal died down when Celtic scored another, and it was the same two players with a long through ball from Roberts finding Sinclair who made it 2–0.

Less than half an hour had gone, and already some Hearts supporters decided that the pub or even a walk round Inverleith Park with their wife or a visit to the castle with their bairns was a better option. They tried to leave and had a bit of a job, apparently, persuading the man on the gate to let them out, for

Brendan Rodgers congratulates Callum McGregor.

he feared that Tynecastle might be invaded by a surge of ticketless Celtic fans if he opened the gate!

Half-time came with the Celtic fans in full voice and everyone expecting more of the same. They duly got it. A trademark goal from Stuart Armstrong from the edge of the box (a feature of this season) was followed by a glorious volley from Patrick Roberts, and then Celtic got a scarcely needed penalty which was duly sunk by Scott Sinclair, who thus notched his hat-trick. Scott Sinclair seemed to like Hearts, for of course it had been at this very ground that he scored his first for the club in the first game of the season, and he had also scored a couple at Celtic Park in January.

Fittingly, towards the end, Brendan brought on some of the fringe players who had also played a part in securing this League title – Christian Gamboa, Gary Mackay-Steven and Kolo Toure, a man whose best playing days were behind him but who had been a great influence behind the scenes. Fittingly, some footage emerged on TV of Kolo Toure leading the Celtic players in the dressing room in the song of homage sung by fans at his previous club to himself and his brother Yaya.

It was a totally fitting way to win a League title, and the superlatives used by the media that day and the following one were totally justified. It was, of course, very easy for people in England to sneer at the poor opposition in Scotland. One has to admit they have a point, but at the same time games still have to be won. And it is hardly the fault of Celtic FC that others can't live with them. You can only play what is put in front of you! In this case, there was the bonus that the team had come to Tynecastle and, frankly, shown everyone the way that football should be played. As those who wrote the Willie Maley song put it, 'he showed them how to play football. He made them the greatest of them all.' Brendan Rodgers was well on his way to doing the same.

It was, of course, remarkable early to win a League. On 2 April there was still an awful lot of football to be played. The temptation must have been to take the foot off the pedal and relax in the remaining eight fixtures – Partick Thistle and Kilmarnock at home, followed by Ross County at Dingwall before the 'split' of another five games, but three things prevented Celtic from doing so. One was the pursuit of records. In particular, we wanted to go through a whole season without being defeated in domestic competition, something that no Celtic team had done before, not even the Lisbon Lions.

The Lisbon Lions themselves provided another incentive. We all knew that it was fifty years ago, and if we were ever likely to forget, the crowd would remind us by their impressive displays in the 67th minute of every game with the lights of mobile phones on, and the words: 'In the heat of Lisbon, the fans came in their thousands, to see the bhoys become Champions 67.' It was good that the fans reminded everyone of these great days, with the underlying message that the players were still expected to live up to such dizzy heights. The players themselves responded.

But the third, and possibly the most important factor was the Scottish Cup and the treble. Winning, like losing, was a habit. We all knew, and had known for some time, that the opponents in the semi-final would be Rangers on 23 April at Hampden, and that the League season, however successful and record-breaking, would nevertheless have more than a hint of anticlimax if we failed to win the Scottish Cup as well. It was important, therefore, to ensure that everyone kept fit and on song for this occasion. We recalled with bitterness and angst last season at a similar stage, where a feckless performance in 120 minutes led to defeat in a penalty shoot-out and was the catalyst for the departure of the likeable, honest, but ultimately 'not-good-enough' Ronnie Deila.

Partick Thistle came to Celtic Park on the Wednesday night immediately after the League was won, and started a tradition, followed honourably by other clubs, of clapping a slightly embarrassed-looking Celtic team, led by Mikael Lustig in the absence of Scott Brown, on to the park to indicate that Celtic were League champions. Partick then settled down to play a good game of football and to show the pundits that they were worthy of the place in the top six that they looked like earning.

No goals in the first half before a slightly sleepy Parkhead, enlivened now and again by the song whose lyrics were none too difficult to remember as they went along the lines of: 'Champions again, oh eh, oh, eh, oh, eh.' The second half brought a little more action, and once again Scott Sinclair was in the middle of it all. In the first place, he picked up a lovely through ball from Patrick Roberts and scored from the right side of the box. Richly did Sinclair deserve the acclaim and the songs that they sang about him, but just as if to prove that the game of football

Christian Gamboa in a game against Hearts at Parkhead.

has a way of bringing someone down to earth, he then missed a penalty. It was a soft penalty brought about when Christian Gamboa was fouled as he crossed for Sinclair, who then tripped over his own feet as he tried to score! Sinclair then took the penalty and shot it straight at the goalkeeper!

In between the goal and the penalty, Partick had equalised through Ade Azeez, and we would have had to admit (charitably, because we had won the League anyway) that Thistle had deserved a point. After all, it is difficult to be churlish and unsympathetic to a loveable bunch of Glasgow boys like Partick Thistle! Apart from a horrible autumn day in 1971, they had never really done us any harm!

Eboue Kouassi was given a start tonight. He showed a few nice touches and clearly was someone to bear in mind for the future, but the significant moment of the night was when he was substituted by Tommy Rogic, a man who was in danger of becoming another 'forgotten man' of Celtic Park. The likeable 'Socceroo' had been out since before the New Year, having an operation on his troublesome ankle. Frankly, given the quality of football played by Celtic at this time, he did not really seem to be badly missed, but he was an added option for Brendan at this time. We would not know until the end of the season just how valuable a part he would play in Celtic's great year.

If Celtic fans were unhappy about just drawing on Wednesday (to their credit, the press did not give us any of the 'How have the mighty fallen!' sort of cant that we have had in the past, notably when Rangers earned a draw a month ago) there was an immediate chance for another win when Kilmarnock came to town on the Saturday. Kilmarnock had struggled this season before chronically poor attendances. They had parted company with their Manager, the likeable Geordie called Lee Clark who was now with Bury. They had replaced him by another Lee, a considerably less likeable character whose surname was McCulloch and who had played, albeit with no great success and with a reputation for doing and saying rather silly things now and again, for Rangers.

Killie would be in the bottom half of the split this season unless they won today and other results went their way. They were unlikely to be relegated, however. In the past they'd had a good record against Celtic at Rugby Park, but often approached Celtic Park as if they were going to the dentist's. But it was another fine day, with even a little heat in the spring sunshine, and a good crowd rolled up, in some cases for their first look at the new champions.

Stuart Armstrong, arguably Celtic's man of the season (he was officially the Man of the Month for March) opened the scoring about halfway through the first half when, with the Kilmarnock defence standing off him, he got the ball about 30 yards from goal and simply shot through a ruck of players to beat the unsighted goalkeeper. Celtic remained on top for the rest of the first half, with the Kilmarnock goalkeeper Freddie Woodman denying them on several occasions.

More was expected in the second half, but it was Kilmarnock who scored rather against the run of play when Jordan Jones beat Craig Gordon with a somewhat fortuitous deflection. It was not likely to last for all that long, however, and Scott

James Forrest with Mikael Lustig in the background.

Sinclair and James Forrest managed to score with tap-ins to give Celtic an easy victory. Moussa Dembele came on as a substitute and was given a great reception from the Parkhead crowd. At the end of the game, the players went over to the supporters and Brendan Rodgers was seen to raise both hands in the air with fingers extended to indicate that he was as keen on 'Ten in a Row' as anyone.

The last scheduled League game before the split was at Dingwall against Ross County on Sunday, 16 April. We knew now that we would have Rangers two weeks in a row (the Scottish Cup and then the Scottish League) on successive weekends, then St Johnstone at home, Aberdeen on a Friday night at Pittodrie, Partick Thistle at Firhill on a Thursday before the final game of the League season against Hearts at Parkhead.

Ross County would be in the lower half of the League following the split, but they were clearly one of the better teams there and they were probably safe enough from relegation. Previous trips to Dingwall had been happy ones, and we had left impressed by the Highland sense of fair play, sportsmanship, courtesy and hospitality. It was a shame that words like 'fair play' could not be said on this occasion, for there was one particularly nasty piece of play-acting that left a sour taste in the mouth, and might have had serious consequences for Celtic.

It concerned a player called Alex Schalk, who had been brought on late in the game when Celtic were 2–1 up. He had clearly been told to do whatever he could to earn a point. He took these instructions far too literally, for I'm sure that Jim McIntyre did not mean him to include cheating (of a pretty basic and blatant variety) in his repertoire. Or if McIntyre did tell him to do that, he clearly underestimated Schalk's ability as an actor. He was what is known in amateur dramatic circles as a 'ham'!

But to begin at the beginning, it was an early start to get to Dingwall for the lunchtime kick-off that Easter Sunday. The sun was once again smiling, and Celtic played well in the first half, playing upfield towards the Ross County supporters. It was Kieran Tierney who opened the scoring just after the half hour mark with a fine low drive from a distance. That was how it was at half-time, but soon after that Ross County equalised when Michael Gardyne headed in a cross from the left, which hit the bar then the line and bounced the wrong way for Celtic, to give the home side a draw which their effort possibly just deserved.

But then, well inside the last quarter of an hour, Patrick Roberts on the right ran through after a clever nutmeg of a County defender and scored with his ever-lethal left foot. The goalkeeper might have done a little better as it squirmed underneath his body and into the net, but full marks to Pat Roberts, one of the clear successes in the latter part of the season.

And that seemed to be that. Celtic indeed hit the bar after that, but then in the last minute of the 90 came the moment that shamed Ross County. Erik Sviatchenko won the ball in his own penalty area and was about to clear it when Alex Schalk, with daylight between him and Sviatchenko, suddenly dived theatrically. I suppose one could say that the angle referee Don Robertson was at was deceptive, but the whole world, including the TV commentators, were absolutely amazed when Mr Robertson pointed to the spot. The dive was amateurish and would not have convinced many people, and quite clearly Sviatchenko did not touch him!

Celtic protested loud and long but Mr Robertson was adamant. His linesman did not help matters, and eventually Celtic realised that arguing with the referee is futile (the referee is always right, even when he is wrong, I was always told) and watched in weary resignation as Liam Boyce converted a penalty to earn his team a point, which was perhaps not entirely undeserved on the merit of how Ross had played, but totally wrong and dishonest in the way the penalty was gained.

This was bad and bad enough, but worse was to follow. Nursing a sense of grievance, Celtic started the minutes of added-on time with renewed vigour, shall we say, and with a little added passion. Too much passion, for Scott Brown's tackle on the same Liam Boyce who had been seen to over-celebrate his penalty conversion was a trifle late. Some referees might have settled for a yellow, but Mr Robertson's judgement may have been affected by his own feeling of guilt and the way that the Ross County players descended on Brown in righteous indignation.

Scott was given the red card, and a real rammy broke out with everyone pushing and shoving one another (as they do in those circumstances, and is usually labelled 'handbags') but order was restored, Scott Brown did indeed leave the field and the game was completed. It was Celtic's fourth and last draw of the season, and there was a nasty feeling of injustice about this.

The result, of course, did not really matter, but what might have been of importance would have been a suspension for our captain Scott Brown if the SFA Disciplinary Committee were to meet before next week's Scottish Cup semi-final. We are terrified that this was going to be the case, and the TV certainly gave that impression, but in fact because of holidays and other things, the meeting was postponed and Broonie was able to play against Rangers. Alex Schalk also had the decency to apologise and to accept a two-match ban for his disgraceful piece of simulation.

In fact, for all the passion raised, it was really much ado about nothing, but what was really important now was the defeat of Rangers in the Scottish Cup semi-final and the visit to Ibrox a week after that. The win in the Scottish Cup was routine and competent; the win at Ibrox was one of our best ever wins there.

The League game on 29 April was approached by Celtic in a reasonably relaxed frame of mind. They had won the Scottish Cup game – and that was the important one. The score at Hampden was 2–0, but that was a poor reflection on the gap between the teams. It should in truth have been a great deal more. Celtic were the clear favourites, therefore, but there was also the feeling that a defeat would be a disappointment, yes, but hardly a heartbreak. The game, in so far as we can say this about any Old Firm game, did not really matter for Celtic. For Rangers, however, there was a feeling of desperation. Clearly their new Manager was going to make changes. Some of the players who had let Warburton down so badly knew they were on their last chance.

As well as desperation, there was also for Rangers the feeling that they were not meant to beat Celtic. It is a feeling that Celtic supporters could identify with, for we had it in the 1960s and again in the 1990s. An inferiority complex is a difficult thing to rid oneself of, particularly when, as here, there is strong evidence to justify such an inferiority complex!

Brendan Rodgers and Pedro Caixinha in a nice sporting gesture.

It turned out to be Celtic's biggest ever win over Rangers at Ibrox. 5–1 had been done at Parkhead more than once, and of course there was the famous 7–1 at Hampden in 1957, but the previous best at Ibrox was 4–0 in season 1897/98 when on 27 September 1897, Celtic, inspired by the immortal Sandy McMahon and Johnny Campbell, gave the 'Light Blues a lesson in football arts' with one of the goals, a header from McMahon being greeted with 'uproarious cheering'.

Today there was indeed a great deal of 'uproarious cheering' from the Broomloan Road end of the ground, and with cause, for Celtic simply ripped them apart, a point conceded by the Ibrox faithful who departed in large numbers long before the game was over. The funny thing was that there was a lack of feeling of exultation that one often gets with a defeat of Rangers. Last week's game had brought that, but now there was a realisation that this Rangers team was a very poor one indeed. It was a fair bet that very few of those wearing the Rangers jersey that day would still be doing so when the new season started.

Naivety was the order of the day for Celtic's first goal. A fellow called Myles Beerman fouled Patrick Roberts, when Roberts was running away from goal to the right but was still in the penalty box. There had been no immediate danger, and the commentators and supporters were all united in their amazement at what on earth he had been thinking of. Scott Sinclair took the penalty kick and Celtic were 1–0 ahead.

Number two came from a very angry-looking Leigh Griffiths (he had a point to prove about team selection, one felt) when he lashed one home after being fed by Stuart Armstrong. There was then a hugely iconic and symbolic picture of Leigh leaning on the corner flag with the Rangers emblem fluttering on it.

It was a source of surprise that Rangers were able to go in at half-time only two down. The chances that Celtic missed would have been a serious source of concern in other circumstances, with Scott Sinclair in particular being prodigal of opportunities as the barrage continued into the second half. Callum McGregor had scored last week through not being picked up, and the same happened this week as Rangers defence once again stood off him and allowed him to fire home number three.

Sporadic cries of 'Seven! Seven!' were heard from the Celtic end, recalling the events of nearly sixty years ago, and this score line was by no means improbable, especially when Dedryck Boyata rose to head home a Griffiths free kick on the right. But then Kenny Miller (oh why did you leave Celtic, Kenny?), the only player in Ibrox colours that day that looked vaguely as if he was worthy of wearing the jersey, pulled one back for Rangers. It was a pity that there were so few Rangers supporters left in the stadium to cheer it, but in any case, Celtic added another through Mikael Lustig near the end.

Little more needed to be said. To their credit, the Rangers fans (apart from the odd one or two isolated incidents) did not react violently to this humiliation, and there were even some of us with a little compassion in our hearts who were able to reflect on just how much they had suffered since their last major honour in 2011. Last year's Scottish Cup Final and the last-minute triumph of Hibs must have been hard to take, and now this year was nothing short of a catastrophe. And yet, six weeks ago when they earned a 1–1 draw against Celtic, the newspapers had unanimously told them what a great team they had! It was hard to work out who were the biggest simpletons – the journalists for writing that sort of rubbish, or the Rangers supporters for believing it!

As far as Celtic were concerned, it was once again 'job done' and now only four League games remained before the game that really mattered – the Scottish Cup Final. Two games were at home – St Johnstone and Hearts – and two away – the short trip to Firhill and then the considerably longer one to Aberdeen for what would be a Cup final rehearsal.

St Johnstone were first on 6 May. Even though there was little at stake for Celtic, it was a good game of football which Celtic won 4–1. St Johnstone had, of course, earned the respect of everyone at Celtic for their fine performances in the previous three encounters that season, and they were working hard to gain the points necessary for Europa League qualification. They also remained the last Scottish side to have beaten Celtic, about a year ago, but they were no match for a rampant Celtic this fine day. Celtic, like the weather, seemed to be getting better and better the longer the season went on, and on this occasion Brendan Rodgers felt able to give two youngsters a taste of the big time.

Tony Ralston played at right-back, and reminded spectators of the way that Kieran Tierney started, showing a maturity away beyond his years, while in the forward line Mike Johnston (whom Rodgers compared to Scott Sinclair) was given a start. There was enough talent there on display to convince the spectators that in addition to any fresh talent that might be bought in over the summer, the supply of talent from the youngsters was not going to dry up any time soon.

It was a good open game, with St Johnstone doing well to keep the score at 0–0 at half-time. But Michael Johnston played a part in Celtic's opener releasing Pat Roberts to finish the job. Scarcely had the applause died down when St Johnstone equalised, Celtic's defence allowing the ball to bob about rather too long in the penalty box without someone using the age-old and tried and tested method of booting it up the park.

But now that Celtic had tasted blood, as it were, the goals began to flow. Dedryck Boyata, who had first shown his heading skills in the first game against St Johnstone at Parkhead back in January, did so here again from a Griffiths corner. Then, Sinclair having replaced Johnston who was given a mighty round of applause, Celtic scored a third. Griffiths shot, the goalkeeper parried and Sinclair was able to get to the ball and turn it back for Roberts to prod homewards. Finally, we had a great goal from the excellent Callum McGregor, who had been given a rest that afternoon, but came on to replace Tommy Rogic and almost immediately scored a great individual goal. The game finished 4–1 but it could just as easily have been double that, and St Johnstone deserved some credit for the way they had played the game as well.

St Johnstone manager Tommy Wright, an Ulstermen with no known affection for Celtic, was full of praise for this Celtic team whom he described as 'exceptional'.

Now with only three League games to go, although, more and more, the word 'invincible' was being heard a shade prematurely, the opinion was beginning to be expressed that Celtic could indeed go through the League season unbeaten. There had been four draws, but not a defeat – and in truth, nothing even vaguely like a defeat. But a vital game and a large hurdle was now looming, in the shape of a game at Pittodrie against Aberdeen on the following Friday night.

The weather was not as good as it had been of late, with rather too much of a North Sea haar hanging over Pittodrie. The crowd was 16,000 and although, if one looked hard enough, one could spot a few empty seats among the Aberdeen support, there were no massive empty spaces of the kind that we had seen rather too often at other grounds this year, and those who were there (and the massive TV audience) saw one of the strangest games of the season.

There were one or two issues to be resolved, even though the League had been well settled some six weeks ago. For one thing, Celtic were trying to preserve their unbeaten record, while Aberdeen were determined to give their supporters something to cheer about. They had last beaten Celtic a year past February on the night that people (some of whom should have known better) predicted the imminent demise of Ronnie Deila's Celtic, perhaps believing the banners which boasted: 'We're coming to get you!'

But the game, while prestigious in itself, was also a rehearsal for the Scottish Cup Final in fifteen days' time. It was an occasion which had excited the normally douce city of Aberdeen, in which football was not always the main topic of conversation, unlike Glasgow, for example, where the working classes very seldom talked about anything else. Everyone seemed determined to go to the Scottish Cup Final, and with Aberdeen's ticket allocation outnumbering their normal home attendance, there seemed to be few problems getting there, however much resentment the ticket allocation caused among Celtic fans!

But how would the teams approach this one? Would they fall into the trap of 'resting' a few players and 'holding back' so as not to give anything away to the Cup Final opponents? Not a bit of it. Celtic were without Scott Brown, but played as if this was the Cup Final itself. And with good cause, for Cup Final places were up for grabs, and competition was keen with so many good players around.

Yet not many people would have predicted the whirlwind start of the Celtic forwards. After 12 minutes, the score was Aberdeen 1 Celtic 3, and then the game settled down. It was actually quite a good game, as well, with both teams coming close to adding to their total, Aberdeen in particular feeling ill done by when a penalty claim was rightly turned down.

Celtic began kicking off to the Beach End and for a while it looked as if Aberdeen were to be swept into the sea. It was Dedryck Boyata who opened the scoring, when he rose majestically to score from a Griffiths corner kick, wisely heading the ball into the ground so that it bounced into the net. That was in three minutes. Five minutes later Callum McGregor shot, the ball rebounded off an Aberdeen defender and Stuart Armstrong rammed in the rebound. Three minutes after that, Leigh Griffiths hammered in another, although goalkeeper Joe Lewis managed to get a hand to it. It has to be said that, well though Celtic were playing, the Aberdeen defence might have done a little better with all three goals, and TV pictures of the Aberdeen crowd behind the goal were quite illuminating with quite a few supporters standing up to demand where was the defence.

But it was not all doom and gloom for the Dons, for almost immediately the talismanic Jonny Hayes scored for them. It was a good goal from a distance, too, not entirely dissimilar to one that he had scored, in different circumstances, in February 2016 on the last occasion that Aberdeen beat Celtic. Then Jayden Stockley headed wide and before half-time Niall McGinn shot straight at Craig Gordon.

'Wow,' said the TV commentators at half-time, and more of the same was expected in the second half, but although the excitement level remained high, there were no further goals. Referee Steven McLean was probably right to refuse Aberdeen a penalty when Craig Gordon came out for the ball and seemed to win it before colliding with Graeme Shinnie. Aberdeen possibly had the edge in pressure but the replacement of Tommy Rogic by the more defensive-minded Nir

Bitton stabilised Celtic, and the game finished 3–1 with both teams getting a great ovation from their fans at the end.

This brought Celtic up to 100 points for the season, and they were now some 30 points ahead of Aberdeen, and Aberdeen had now lost four times to Celtic this season. How this affects players, we do not know. While complacency must at all costs be avoided, success does seem to convince the winning team that they can win the next game as well. On the other hand, Aberdeen being such a good team, one felt that they had to beat Celtic some time and Aberdeen fans clearly believed that the Cup Final was the time for this to happen.

And yet, looking at that Celtic side, it was still hard to spot a weakness. Tonight at Pittodrie had seen Celtic rampant and scoring three goals in 11 minutes. They had passed that test, but then they had been put to another test. This was the equally difficult one of defending against a team which contained men like Hayes McGinn, and latterly Rooney. Celtic had passed that test as well, and had looked a very complete team. And all that without Scott Brown!

Firhill was the venue for the penultimate League game on a warm Thursday night. Frankly, this game was too one-sided to be anything of a contest, and Celtic finished up winning 5–0 with the highlight of the night, as much as the football, being the display of flags, banners and the constant singing to remind everyone, in case we had forgotten, that next Thursday night would be the fiftieth anniversary of Lisbon. It was a rare opportunity for an old-timer like myself to see how the Green Brigade worked. In remarkable unison with each other and with the love of the club clearly and indelibly written on their faces, they were a crowd that any club would love to have. Indefatigable and constant, the noise was tremendous throughout, and the young man banging the drum hardly saw the game at all. He had a job to do!

Patrick Roberts was superb throughout, with two great goals, Tommy Rogic got a fairly lucky one which went in off both posts and which he had the decency to smile about, Callum McGregor got one that came down off the bar and was given by the eagle-eyed linesman whose judgement was subsequently proved to be correct, and Leigh Griffiths, who had scored the first goal with a penalty kick, threw a mini-tantrum when he was taken off. This 'questioning of the Manager's decision', one presumes, led to a stern word or two from Mr Rodgers, but was rightly made light of, in spite of the media trying to make more of it than it was, for it was a welcome sign of Griffiths wanting to be more in the action!

The night was slightly spoiled by the road to the motorway being closed because of a murder or something (never!) and a long detour before we got home, but we now only had Hearts at Parkhead on Sunday standing in the way of an unbeaten League record. Frankly, we had grounds for confidence.

In fact, it was party, party, party all the time at a packed Celtic Park that Sunday. Those of us who remembered last year and the seven goals dished out to the hapless Motherwell wondered if the same might happen, but in fact we restricted ourselves to two, a header from Griffiths and a drive from Armstrong. These goals were almost incidental to the main business which was, of course, the presentation of the trophy.

The team had now played 38 League games, won 34 and drawn 4, giving them a total of 106 points out of a possible 114. They had also scored 106 goals and beaten their nearest challengers, Aberdeen, by 30 points. It was almost otiose to go on. We had been privileged to see a great season, not as good as 1967 or 1908 when we won absolutely everything, but certainly in that top bracket. We might yet blow up in next Saturday's Scottish Cup Final, but for the moment we had nothing else to do but enjoy the celebrations.

Loads of pyrotechnics and ticker tape followed, and the thing was very well orchestrated, the highlights perhaps being the appearance of Kris Commons, a man who had fallen badly out of favour with Ronnie Deila and had subsequently been prevented by injury from getting back with Brendan Rodgers. But he had been a great player for the club – one of those many who were not necessarily born to love the Celtic, as so many of us were, but who loved them now.

And then there was the appearance of the wives and children. How humbling it was to see so many of the wives and children of foreign origin walking round to take the plaudits along with their husbands! Possibly they had never heard of Celtic before, but they had now! This day would stay with them, as it would with all of us, for the rest of their lives. Never, surely, had there been more convincing proof of the mantra of Brother Walfrid, repeated so often by Willie Maley, that 'it is not a man's creed or nationality that counts, it's the man himself!'

And the children – 'toddlin' stacher through to meet their Dad, wi' flichterin' noise and glee' as they did in Robert Burns' 'The Cotter's Saturday Night', all decked in the green and white and relishing the occasion every bit as much as the boys and girls on the terracing! Once again, we had to reckon that this was indeed 'the greatest show on earth'.

And then, just as we were about to leave, we noticed that in the away section there were a group of supporters, possibly about ten of them, who had stayed to clap. Perhaps they were pro-Celtic infiltrators among the Hearts support, perhaps they were some of the many (there are more such people than one thinks!) who simply love good football and found it easier to get into the Hearts section than the Celtic one, or perhaps they were genuine Hearts supporters who were decent enough to admit that Celtic in 2017 were quite simply a great team. Whoever they were, God bless them!

CHAPTER **THIRTEEN**
THE SCOTTISH CUP

The Scottish Cup is the trophy that one has associated most with Celtic over the years. Yes, Lisbon was more prestigious, and the Scottish League is more important in that it can lead to the Champions League, but the Scottish Cup is the one that, in some ways, defines Celtic's season. As this year's competition began, we had won it thirty-six times, and what a host of memories it could stir in us – the very first Scottish Cup win in 1892, an occasion which had as great an effect on the Celtic community of its day as the European Cup did in 1967, Jimmy Quinn's great hat-trick of 1904, Patsy Gallacher's demolition of Hibs on the eve of the Great War, the same Patsy's epic and scarcely believable goal in 1925, the comeback against Motherwell in 1931, the world record crowd in 1937, Billy McNeill's great winner in 1965, the contemptuous sweeping aside of Rangers in 1969, Dixie Deans' hat-trick in 1972, twice coming back from the dead against Dundee United in the 1980s, and Henrik Larsson in 2001 and 2004 – all these are woven into the Celtic psyche.

By the same token, this trophy has given us heartbreaks as well. Those of us old enough will recall the scarring of our childhoods and adolescence by the awful four Cup Final defeats in 1955, 1956, 1961 and 1963. We were outclassed in 1956 (although a question or two was asked about some of the Celtic defending) and in the other three, we should have won the first games but let them go to disastrous replays. In all four, there was a faulty team selection, and all four provided us with some 'unspeakable grief' as Aeneas says to Dido.

The Scottish Cup is a remarkable success story, and has been since its first tie was played in 1873/74 (the trophy pre-dates Celtic by well over a decade) and although the FA Cup (or, as we call it, the English Cup) is a couple of years older, the venerable old trophy that one sees in the Hampden Museum (well worth a visit, incidentally) is the oldest in world football, so old that it can only be presented to the winners before it is replaced by a replica for the winning captain to take on its lap of honour and keep for a year. Thirty-six times, as we say, the Scottish Cup had made its way to Celtic Park. Could Brendan Rodgers and company make it thirty-seven?

There are two good quiz questions about the Scottish Cup. One is, which team comes third in the total of most wins, behind Celtic and Rangers? Unless you ask this question of someone who knows a certain amount about Victorian football, it will be a while before anyone comes up with Queen's Park, and once, famously, Jock Stein did not know that! The other is what have Queen's Park, Vale of Leven, Rangers and Aberdeen done with the Scottish Cup that Celtic haven't? And the answer is that they have won the trophy three years in a row, something that Celtic, for all their prolific success in the Scottish Cup, have yet to achieve. They might have done it in 1901, but goalkeeper Dan McArthur had a shocker, they might have done it in 1909 but the fans rioted, and they might have done it in 1990 but they lost in a heart-breaking penalty shoot-out to Aberdeen. So, while we look for ten League championships in a row, we could also be doing with three-in-a-row Scottish Cups.

The secret of the Scottish Cup has always been its essential simplicity. Not the least exciting part of the Scottish Cup is the draw now made live on TV. There has been a little tinkering with the early rounds over the years, including, in recent years, the admission of what we used to call Junior clubs, but by the time that Celtic enter the competition, it is a straight draw with the SFA laudably resisting any idea of seeding with the intention of cooking things for a Rangers v. Celtic final. Cynics may say that has happened anyway, pointing to the fact that Celtic and Rangers between them have now won the trophy seventy times, but on the other hand, since the turn of the century teams like Dundee United, Inverness Caledonian Thistle and St Johnston have all had their moment of glory. That cannot but be good for Scottish football.

On the other hand, Celtic fans are generally interested in the success of their own club rather than the common good. Mind you, in 2016, there was the rare example of Celtic fans shouting at their TV screens in support of another team in the Scottish Cup Final. The other team were Hibs – and of course the origins of both clubs were similar, with Hibs sometimes being contemptuously referred to as 'the Edinburgh branch' by those who found common Irish heritage a problem – but there was also the fact that Hibs in 2016 hotched with ex-Celts – Dylan McGeough, Anthony Stokes and Manager Alan Stubbs, and of course Liam Henderson, that grossly underrated player, was with Hibs on loan. Added to the fact that the opponents were the apparently revivified Rangers, and there was no excuse for not supporting the green and whites of the other big Scottish city that day.

You couldn't have said that Hibs had exactly dominated the Scottish Cup. They had won it twice – in 1887 (and that was one of the catalysts for the founding of Celtic later that year, in that, if the Edinburgh Irish could win the Scottish Cup, why couldn't a Glasgow Irish team do likewise?) and in 1902 when they beat Celtic with a back-heeler from a man called Andy McGeachen, but since then it had been total failure with Celtic through Patsy Gallacher, Joe Cassidy, Dixie Deans, Henrik Larsson and Gary Hooper wrecking their Cup Final hopes on many occasions.

They looked as if they were going to blow up again in 2016, for they were 2–1 down until late in the game, when Liam Henderson took these two corner kicks and 'Hibs' and the 'Scottish Cup' could now be mentioned again in the same breath. Sadly, some less than totally intelligent spectators decided to have a fight on the pitch, but nevertheless it had been a good Scottish Cup Final for Celtic supporters and we looked forward with anticipation to the draw for the 2017 competition.

The draw was held on a Monday night in late November at Rugby Park, and Celtic were paired with Albion Rovers away from home. It was a shame that Celtic supporters were denied the opportunity to visit Cliftonhill, that derelict old lady of a stadium, where one would definitely have seen football in the raw, but any rational look at things would have seen the logistic problems, and after a certain amount of toing and froing, the game was arranged for the Shyberry Excelsior Stadium, the home of Airdrie. Celtic fans were familiar with this ground, for they had played there last year against East Kilbride in a game which singularly failed to excite anyone's imagination.

Albion Rovers are a club that one has to admire. By any method of reckoning, they should really have disappeared long ago like Bathgate, Broxburn, Leith Athletic, Third Lanark and Clydebank, but good management and stewardship, along with the determination of men like Tom Fagan, had ensured that this team did not go under. The town of Coatbridge, by any standard a Celtic-supporting stronghold, is very close to Glasgow, but the Rovers have preserved their own identity and kept going.

One would look in vain for any sustained glory from Albion Rovers throughout their long history since 1882, but they did reach the Final of the Scottish Cup of 1920, that chaotic season where everything took such a long time to settle down after the war, only to lose narrowly to Kilmarnock in the Final after they had beaten Aberdeen and Rangers en route! They finished bottom of the League that season as well! In the war years, they gave an opportunity to a young miner called Jock Stein, a man who was a 'Bevin Boy' producing the much-needed coal for the war effort rather than fighting overseas, and there was also a fine player called Tony Green in the 1960s who went on to play for Newcastle United and Scotland, but apart from that, success and Albion Rovers have not exactly gone hand in hand. In January 2017, they were struggling near the bottom of Division One, the third tier. (How can Division One be the third tier, do I hear you ask?)

Celtic's game against Albion Rovers was to be televised, a welcome boost to the coffers of the wee Rovers, and was arranged for Sunday, 22 January. It would be the first game after the midwinter shutdown, a phenomenon which was not always well liked by the fans. Thus, by the time that Celtic took the field against the Rovers, Celtic's main rivals Rangers and Aberdeen were already through to the next round, Rangers having come from behind to beat Motherwell in a somewhat depressing TV game the day before. Aberdeen had dispatched Stranraer 4–0, Hibs had beaten Bonnyrigg Rose to the tune of 8–1, while Hearts, who were on TV just before the Celtic game, had victory snatched from them by a late Raith Rovers equaliser.

The weather was cold and raw, but the virtually full stadium of 8,319 spectators provided a good atmosphere for what was Celtic's first game since Hogmanay when they beat Rangers. There was never, I suppose, any great doubt about who the eventual winners were going to be, although the all-weather pitch at Airdrie, like all pitches of that ilk, took a little getting used to. It was good to see Kieran Tierney back for his first game since October, and although he was wisely taken off after about an hour in order to break him in gently, we saw enough to remind us of just what we had been missing.

Celtic scored about the half hour mark with a chip from Scott Sinclair on the edge of the box. It looked for all the world as if it were going to hit the bar or sail harmlessly over, but Scott had judged it perfectly so that it entered the net at the very corner. Those who expected a deluge of goals were to be disappointed, for Albion Rovers stuck to their task very well and thwarted Celtic up to half-time and well into the second half. Celtic, clearly struggling with the artificial pitch and the effects of the lay-off, took their time. Quite a few chances went a-begging, but eventually in the 77th minute Scott Brown cut one back from the right and Dembele was on hand to do the needful. Thirteen minutes later, and virtually at the end of the regulation 90 minutes, Stuart Armstrong added a third to ensure that Celtic would be in the draw for the next round at the end of the game.

The making of the draw for the next round of the Scottish Cup is normally a staid, stylised, stilted and stiff sort of affair with a pompous official saying Mr 'so and so' will draw the home team and Mr 'someone else' will draw the away team. It is not unheard of for mistakes to be made and everyone having to start again, as had happened embarrassingly in front of TV cameras last year. Not this time, however, for in a welcome innovation, the SFA invited Rod Stewart, pop singer, to do the needful. Rod was, of course, an unashamed Celtic (and Scotland) supporter and had attended the game before making the draw, being seen talking to the fans in the crowd before he did so.

Alan Stubbs, ex-Manager of Hibs, and of course the last Manager to win the Cup, was there to help as well, but it was Rod Stewart who stole the show with his rather eccentric method of diving into the urn to bring out each team. Some traditionalists were horrified at all that, but most people saw it as a laugh. The draw managed to keep Celtic, Rangers and Aberdeen apart but the best tie of the round was, of course, the Edinburgh derby at Tynecastle. Celtic had the task of facing Inverness Caledonian Thistle at Celtic Park. The weaker among us might have remembered the year 2000 and recoiled, but this was a different Celtic and, indeed, a different Inverness.

A more recent painful Scottish Cup memory was, of course, the 2015 semi-final. That was the day we met referee Steven McLean, who made a howler by missing a fairly obvious hand-ball, and then reduced us to ten men by sending off Craig Gordon. Inverness went on to win the Scottish Cup that year, but they were not doing so well now, and even though Griffiths and Armstrong were out injured, it was confidently expected that Celtic would drive them back up the A9, hammered and chastened, in this early Saturday kick-off on 11 February.

Possibly there was some kind of a protest at the early kick-off, for only 25,577 turned up at Celtic Park, a good 30,000 below what one would expect for a League game. There were reasons for this – the main one being that it was not included in the season ticket package and you had to pay for it! The fact that the game was on TV was also a factor, it was a cold raw February day, spring not as yet anywhere near Celtic Park, and there were also quite real logistic factors in supporters who lived in Ireland, England or the more remote parts of Scotland getting there in time for an early kick-off.

But whether one watched the game on TV or in the flesh, it was a marvellous Celtic performance as the Highlanders were torn apart 6–0, and it really should have been an awful lot more. Most unusually, Celtic started kicking off to the Jock Stein Stand, but it hardly made a huge amount of difference. James Forrest started off well on song, and arguably played his best ever game for the club. The first goal scorer was, of all people, Mikael Lustig, who turned brilliantly to put Celtic ahead. Then, for the second week in a row, Moussa Dembele scored a hat-trick (he had done similarly last week against St Johnstone at Perth) before Kieran Tierney scored the fifth – a very popular goal that one was! – and even more welcomed by the Celtic support was the one scored by Scott Brown who then faced the Lisbon Lions stand and did his own 'Broonie' impersonation of himself!

Small crowd or not, it was a very happy one at this performance. Granted, the opposition was not great, but there seemed to be no reason to believe that this side could not now go on to add the Scottish Cup to the Scottish League Cup which was already theirs, and the Scottish League which was now only a matter of time. In the meantime, we settled back on our buses, happy with the ways of the world and awaiting the other results in the Scottish Cup, content in the knowledge that we at least were in the last eight.

That afternoon, Partick Thistle, St Mirren and Aberdeen joined us. Aberdeen were, by the admission of very many of their supporters, lucky to get the better of Ross County by 1–0 at Dingwall. There were two draws – Dunfermline v. Hamilton and Ayr United v. Clyde (Ayr United and Hamilton would eventually win through in the replays), and on the Sunday we settled ourselves in front of the TV to watch the Edinburgh derby and then to cheer on Greenock Morton when they took on Rangers. The game at Tynecastle was goalless and disappointing in terms of quality football, if not in effort (Hibs would win the replay at Easter Road) and from our unbiased perspective, Greenock Morton had really bad luck at Ibrox after scoring first.

Rangers had sacked Mark Warburton on Friday (we could now go back to buying a loaf of Warburton's bread in the supermarket without feeling traitorous!) and we hoped that Morton could take advantage of this, but their forwards were profligate of chances, with a couple late on in particular that should have been put away, and Rangers were through with the draw taking place at Ibrox immediately after the game and being done by Alec McLeish. No complaints about Big Eck this time – he gave us a home tie against Championship strugglers St Mirren! Once again, the big boys avoided each other.

St Mirren were a team who had fallen on bad times of late, but they were a club whose tradition in the Scottish Cup was second to none of the provincial teams.

They had won the trophy on three occasions, in 1926, 1959 and 1987, and many times they had been the death of Celtic. They had defeated us in the mysterious final of 1926 when, to use a modern phrase, Celtic, League champions and playing brilliantly, 'simply didn't turn up'. Adam McLean was injured and that seemed to have an undue effect on the rest of the team, with Tommy McInally in particular having an off day. Then there were these two awful semi-finals of 1959 and 1962, when Celtic were simply hammered to an extent that the supporters couldn't accept, and in 1962 turned very nasty in some sort of misguided attempt to get the game replayed. As recently as 2009, St Mirren had put us out of the Scottish Cup at the quarter-final stage.

Against that, there had been that glorious Scottish Cup Final of 1908 with Jimmy McMenemy on song, a very tight 1–0 win at a dangerously overcrowded Love Street in 1963, an epic replay at the same venue in 1980 when the crowd was similarly tight and uncomfortable, and a rather uninspiring semi-final at Hampden in 1984 in the wind and the rain, but it did produce a positive result.

St Mirren had never been the same since they left the old Love Street, a quaint old ground with loads of character and history. For us, of course, there are the happy memories of the 'Albert Kidd' day in the rain in 1986. However, 3 May 1986 was not all about Albert. Celtic's first half performance that day will live in the memory for long, and if they had played anything like that earlier in the season, they would have won a domestic treble with a degree of ease. On the other hand, there was that awful night at the new St Mirren stadium in March 2010 when a 0–4 thrashing was the catalyst for the axe for the luckless Tony Mowbray who, likeable man though he was, was simply not up to the awesome demands of the job.

Celtic were scheduled for lunchtime on Sunday, 5 March. By that time, we knew that last year's finalists were through to the semi-finals, Rangers having thrashed a weak and disappointing Hamilton side 6–0 at Ibrox, and Hibs having a little more difficulty in getting the better of Ayr United at Easter Road. St Mirren, by any standards, were having a poor season. Ill supported by the town of Paisley, they had a good Manager in Jack Ross, but he had inherited a very poor squad and this season was a perpetual battle against relegation from the Championship into Division One. They eventually succeeded in retaining their status, and indeed reached the Final of the Championship Challenge Trophy, but no one will say that 2016/17 was a vintage season for the Buddies.

But today at Parkhead, in front of another disappointing crowd of 27, 455, who impressively stood in silence for Tommy Gemmell who had died during the week, St Mirren with nothing to lose and rather enjoying the media attention (being on TV was a rare event for the Buddies) played a good first half, and a major seismic shock was feared when half-time was reached with St Mirren 1–0 up! The goal

Gary Mackay-Steven.

had come from a free kick, headed down by John Sutton (brother of Chris) into the path of Harry Davis (a man with the same name as a Rangers player of the early 1960s, but presumably no relation) who put St Mirren one up.

Celtic took off Gary Mackay-Steven, who was not having his best game, and replaced him with Patrick Roberts. It would be nice to say that the effect was dramatic and instantaneous, but in fact it wasn't, and indeed St Mirren might well have gone two up when a ball was driven into the Celtic penalty area, hit Dembele (of all people!) and bounced up to hit the bar and come down on the right side of the line, just out of the reach of a St Mirren forward. One would have had to admit that Celtic were lucky there.

It would have been difficult for Celtic to come back from that but, as it happened, Celtic then scored twice in a few minutes, added a third 10 minutes later before Leigh Griffiths finished it all off with a fourth. The first came from Mikael Lustig when he headed home a Roberts free kick, and then with the Paisley defence still struggling to come to terms with that one, Scott Sinclair showed just why he is so highly rated by the Celtic supporters. With several St Mirren defenders between him and the goal as he ran towards them on the left, he suddenly, with the side of his foot, curled home a shot into the roof of the net. Simple!

There is simply no answer to that one and Sinclair was also involved in the third goal, teaming up well with Patrick Roberts to give Dembele a simple tap in. That made it three, Griffiths added a fourth before the end and we all wondered what on earth the fuss had been about at half-time when all the pundits (including, apparently, those who should have known a great deal better) were talking of a 'shock'! Nevertheless, St Mirren were given a good round of applause from the Parkhead crowd, who felt that St Mirren really should be a Premier League club.

Celtic were now into the semi-finals. So too were Aberdeen, who beat Partick Thistle (not without a struggle) at Pittodrie to join Rangers and Hibs. We thus had the three favourites plus last season's winners, and with everyone on social media happy to make a fool of themselves yet again with statements like 'Celtic and Rangers will be kept apart for the Final', the draw was conducted with stunning impartiality by Alex Smith, who had managed Cup-winning sides in 1987 and 1990, along with our very own Bertie Auld, and Celtic were paired with Rangers.

Some felt that Celtic got the easiest draw there! It didn't matter, for there is no such thing as an easy draw, particularly at the semi-final stage. The games were scheduled for 22/23 April (six weeks hence) with Celtic and Rangers on the Sunday, while Hibs and Aberdeen were on the Saturday. Both were lunchtime kick-offs and both would be televised.

A Celtic v. Rangers game needs no extra build-up, but we had bitter memories of last year at the same stage and that heart-breaking penalty shoot-out which signalled the end of Ronnie Deila. This year was different, however. The League was already won by some distance and if anyone needed to be reminded of the disparity between the two teams, all he had to do was to look at the League table. And yet, it was the Scottish Cup, where anything could happen. We had fallen at the semi-final hurdle in 2010, 2012, 2015 and 2016, and on each of these four occasions, we had been the favourites. There was no place for complacency.

But before we psyched ourselves up to going to Hampden on Sunday, there was the other semi-final to be enjoyed on TV on the Saturday. And 'enjoy' was the word, for it was a fine game, although we would have preferred Hibs to win. Surprisingly, Aberdeen hadn't been to a Scottish Cup Final since the year 2000, but they reached the Final today, even though they squandered a two-goal lead. But Hibs still had their own Scottish Cup death wish about them. With a little more conviction, they might have won, but as it happened they conceded a late goal from a wicked deflection, something which happened too late in the game for them to counteract. We did, however, have the spectacle of Hibs goalkeeper Ofir Marciano joining the attack and almost scoring with a late header, which was saved by the other goalkeeper Joe Lewis.

The crowd at this game was a disappointing 31,969. Celtic supporters would get angry about this when they discovered that Aberdeen would have as many supporters as we did at the Final, but in fairness it must be pointed out that getting from Aberdeen for a lunchtime start at Hampden was no easy option. One accepts that a televised game shouldn't be played at the same time as other games, but surely there is a strong case for making a semi-final involving Aberdeen kick-off at 5.30 p.m. if it is to be played at Hampden. This would have allowed more Aberdeen supporters to get there. The sad thing is that Hampden, inadequate though it is, is still better than anywhere else. Tynecastle or Murrayfield might have helped Hibs fans, but it would not really have solved the problems for the Dons.

So, Aberdeen awaited the winners on the Sunday. Not everyone likes the atmosphere at Old Firm games, and at Hampden there is certainly a problem with parking on such occasions, but the place was full, as one would have expected, and one often feels that one of the problems with Hampden is that it is simply not big enough. The crowd of 50,000 could easily have been doubled.

Celtic were at full strength for this game, with Dembele preferred up front to Griffiths – but not for long, because Dembele picked up what looked like a hamstring and had to be replaced by Griffiths in the 34th minute. This did not exactly weaken Celtic, and, interestingly, in the same way as Dembele played a large part in the first goal, so too was Griffiths influential in the second.

Celtic kicked off playing to the Rangers end of the ground, and very soon had put down a marker. They were faster to the ball, they looked more in command of the game on what must have been a very nervous occasion for all players – it certainly was to all spectators! – and in 10 minutes we took the lead. A long ball from the very influential Mikael Lustig found Dembele who, intelligently, did not try to score himself, but cut the ball back to Callum McGregor who placed the ball perfectly from about 20 yards. It was a very well taken goal, and the Celtic end was a sea of appreciation.

Rangers, who had not yet lost a game under Pedro Caixinha, came back into the game to a certain extent but were extremely lucky to finish the half with eleven men still on the field, when a strong case could have been made for them being reduced to nine. The TV and radio commentators shared this opinion as well as the Celtic end, and it certainly seemed that Willie Collum, never in the past reluctant to brandish red cards, 'bottled it' on two occasions.

One was when Andy Halliday committed a dreadful tackle on Patrick Roberts, whom Rangers clearly were targeting as the danger man. It was a shocker, a potential leg breaker, and does not get any nicer the oftener one sees it on YouTube. It was a straight red card, one felt, and could hardly be excused on the grounds that Halliday was a 'full blooded Rangers supporter' as a member of the press tried ludicrously to explain it away the following day!

And then Miles Beerman was rightly booked for his attentions on Patrick Roberts – but kept on fouling! Fortunately, Celtic were professional enough not to let this distract them from the job in hand, and hurt Rangers where it was really sore – by beating them on the park.

The half-time whistle came with Celtic 1–0 up and well on top. The phrase 'well on top' does not, of course, mean very much, for such things can change rapidly. But then, five minutes into the second half, Celtic went further ahead via the penalty spot when Leigh Griffiths, running in on goal, was brought down by James Tavernier and Mr Collum had no hesitation in pointing to the spot. The penalty was given to Scott Sinclair who, very calmly, picked his spot to the goalkeeper's right. It was not the cleanest of penalties for the ball hit the post first and then entered the net.

There are those of us who worry about a 2–0 scoreline. It should be enough with 40 minutes to go, but sometimes it isn't. Hampden has a big screen with the time on it, and I would have to admit that I sneaked more than a few looks at it during the next 40 minutes. Rangers did rally a little, forcing Craig Gordon into at least three good saves, but Celtic missed a few chances as well and the feeling grew that even if Rangers did get one back, Celtic could without any great difficulty up a gear and deal with them. By about the 80th minute, Rangers began to look a beaten team and unlikely to make any great impression on the excellent Celtic back four of Lustig, Simunovich, Boyata and Tierney, with those who used to say that Boyata would never make it looking more than a little silly now. 'It doesn't matter, cos we've got Boyata' began to make an appearance in the supporters' repertoire.

Full time came and Celtic were now into their 56th Scottish Cup Final, the previous 55 having consisted of 36 wins, 18 defeats and 1 withholding of the Cup because of the 1909 riot. It was another great triumph for Brendan Rodgers, who behaved throughout the game with a dignity and a calm demeanour that perhaps belied his inner tension. Inner tension was certainly evident in the support as well but at full time our joy knew no bounds. Indeed, it was a double victory in that Celtic were in the Final, and Rangers weren't. Those who are not in this system often scratch their heads and wonder at the passion of it all, but that is just the way that it is.

So, as Celtic went from strength to strength, Rangers' season began to fizzle out. When they qualified for the Europa League a few weeks later, they celebrated with disproportionate glee. It was, however, obvious that under the ambitious Portuguese gentleman called Pedro Caixinha things were, going to change and that the exit door would be shown to some of their players who had served them well in the lower divisions, but had clearly reached the limit of their ability.

Once again, we compared the two clubs. Rangers had been in charge (they had also had a great deal of luck) some twenty years ago – some of our support argue that was a different club altogether – but their methods had been false and pregnant with the seeds of their future destruction, whereas Celtic were now properly run and a model for other clubs. No dodgy deals, no illegal payments and the income tax being paid to HMRC on time! But oh, what a bitter legacy had been left to Rangers supporters by those who used to run that club!

But moving on from the tribal stuff, it was Celtic v. Aberdeen for the final. Celtic had won the Cup thirty-six times to Aberdeen's seven. There had been six direct Scottish Cup Finals between the two of them and the 'score' was 3–3. Celtic had won 2–1 before a world record attendance in 1937, before a crowd that was only slightly less in 1954 and by the same score, and while en route to Lisbon in 1967, as it were, we had beaten the Dons 2–0 with two Willie Wallace goals on each side of half-time. Aberdeen's three victories had all left a bad taste in the mouth. There had been bad refereeing from Bobby Davidson in 1970, a couple of controversial decisions in 1984 as well, and then the 1990 Scottish Cup Final had been won on a penalty shoot-out, which even Aberdeen players and fans agreed was no way to settle the venerable Scottish Cup. But, of course, a penalty shoot-out is good television and even as far back as 1990, it was all, very sadly, about money.

As far as 2017 was concerned, although Celtic were considered to be far and away the favourites, there was little doubt that Aberdeen on a good day could beat them. They had some good players, notably Jonny Hayes. Celtic, on the other hand, had better men in almost every position, it was felt, and as long as nothing stupid happened, the Scottish Cup would be theirs to collect. Patrick Roberts, still only on loan from Manchester City, actually turned down an opportunity to play in the England Under-20 team in order to play for Celtic in the Scottish Cup Final, something that, as well as going down extraordinarily favourably in Celtic circles, also sent out a message to everyone in England that here at least was one player who rated Scottish football very highly.

Celtic fielded their strongest team, and that allowed them to keep Dembele, Rogic and Forrest on the bench! Dembele had been out with an injury but was now fit again, but Leigh Griffiths was still given the nod. Aberdeen, in a move which caused some argument among their supporters, sacked Ryan Jack from the captaincy after he had unwisely let it be known that he was about to join Rangers for next season! And yet he was still playing for Aberdeen, but not as captain!

The weather was very hot with heavy showers of rain alternating with periods of almost unbearable sunshine, and thunder and lightning not very far away. Indeed, at a key point of the game lightning forked over Hampden. Now what would some civilizations have made of that? Whose side were the gods on? The teams came out to very impressive colour displays from both sets of supporters, although the Aberdeen rallying cry to 'Stand Free' seemed to be campaigning for free entrance to football games and no more seating! There certainly was not a lot of seating at the Celtic end, for everyone seemed to have decided to stand.

Aberdeen started towards the Celtic end, and it was they who took the lead. A corner on the right was taken by Niall McGinn and it sailed over everyone until Jonny Hayes suddenly got away from Leigh Griffiths, who had been detailed to mark him, ran in and scored to a huge eruption of sound from the Mount Florida End. It had been an easily preventable goal, but within a few minutes it had been counteracted when Callum McGregor, even when being fouled, managed to slip the ball to Stuart Armstrong who scored one of his trademark goals from outside the penalty box. And that is how it remained until half-time, although Scott Sinclair should have scored another for Celtic just before the whistle went.

It had been a pretty even first half, although Celtic had suffered the loss of Kieran Tierney with what looked like a broken jaw after a collision (accidental, one hopes) with the elbow of Jayden Stockley. TV pictures were inconclusive as to intent, although not everyone was prepared to give Stockley the benefit of the doubt. It was, however, a bad injury and Kieran was taken to hospital. It was interesting to note the substitution. It was the man for all seasons, the Wizard of Oz, Tommy Rogic, the utility man. The rest of the game would show just how useful the Australian would be.

The second half saw some tremendous football from Celtic, as they gradually gained control of the game with the midfield of Scott Brown, Callum McGregor and in particular Patrick Roberts seizing the initiative. Scott Sinclair was playing well enough up to the penalty area, but had several culpable misses, one in particular that he put over the bar. Patrick Roberts hit the post. Dedryck Boyata, whose defensive work was impeccable, came up for a corner, got a clean header but missed the chance. Against that, Aberdeen had the occasional breakaway and a bad and rare error from Callum McGregor gave them an opportunity which McLean should have made more of.

There was never a dull moment in this game, a point conceded by the English and European press covering the game. A thunderstorm was in progress – apparently, and I say that because no one in the stadium really noticed, so engrossed were we all in the game and we were all under cover. What would it have been like on the huge open terracings of Hampden in the old days, one wonders?

Celtic kept plugging away, winning several corners on the left, most of which were taken by Leigh Griffiths who gestured to the support for more encouragement, something that was hardly necessary for the crowd were in full cry. Confidence grew, and yet there was the nagging thought that this competent Aberdeen side might yet seize upon a moment of opportunity and win the day. Such things did happen in Cup Finals and they happened to Celtic. Those of us old enough recalled 1961.

The 90 minutes had now gone, and we were playing the three added minutes, but reconciled to extra time. Penalties we did not want, for Celtic usually do badly on such occasions – the 1990 Cup Final against today's opponents or, perhaps worse, last year's semi-final sprung to mind – but then up stepped Tommy Rogic. the wily Australian, in and out of the side this season and plagued with injury, picked up a ball about halfway inside the Aberdeen half. Realising that some of the Aberdeen defenders were tired and longing for the haven of full time and a respite, he charged at them, and through them to reach the six yard line. He might have cut the ball back – but that was what everyone expected him to do, and he also twigged that Sinclair and Griffiths were having an off day in front of goal and might have sclaffed the ball over the bar – so he simply had a go himself, transferring the ball from his left to his right foot to score.

The goal itself is, of course, available to watch on YouTube, but I think that the best commentary I have heard is the one on Celtic TV with the emotion of the commentator mirroring the attitude of the fans. No attempt at impartiality or anything like that, just sheer hysteria, while poor Jim Craig, suffering from a bad cold, does his best to pour a little sanity and restraint on the proceedings. But it had nothing to do with sanity!

How hard it is to describe or even to comprehend the following few minutes. Ecstatic, delirious, rapturous, confused as complete strangers hugged, kissed and gave each other high-fives. It was total, orgasmic, Celtic joy with the feeling that this was what life was all about. Not all our supporters enjoyed great fortune in their private lives...but they did in their public green and white existence. They were once again the risen people! Or, as it was more crudely put, 'The Rangers and the Tories could go and f***! Our bhoys have won the Cup!'

Tommy Rogic, the Wizard of Oz.

And you almost sensed the presence of the dead generations of Celtic fans who had perhaps enjoyed 1892 or 1925 coming to join us now. To my certain knowledge, my father and grandfather joined me for a second, as did my grandchildren sitting watching TV in their Aberdeen (yes, Aberdeen – but they were draped in green and white!) home. The past, the present and the future were all joined together in one glorious Celtic moment.

On a more worldly level, there was still a minute or so to see out. Whenever anyone scores a Cup Final goal these days, they always go to the corner on the right to kiss a fan or two. Hibs did it last year, and we did it this year. It took a while to disentangle Rogic and we now had to hold out. In fact, Aberdeen mounted an attack and might have equalised, but did not quite get a touch on it to divert the ball past Craig Gordon, who was fouled as he smothered the ball and lay on the ground with it. Seconds later, after the ball was kicked up the park, referee Bobby Madden (who actually had a good game) pointed to the stand, and yet again, and for the thirty-seventh time, our bhoys had won the Cup.

Leaving aside the treble and the fact that Celtic could now with justification be called 'the invincibles', this was yet another epic Celtic Scottish Cup win, featuring, apart from anything else, an ability to come from behind, and to score a late goal to drape the Scottish Cup with green and white ribbons, surely the most glorious sight in world football. 2017 thus takes its place among the great Scottish Cup years, joining 1892, 1899, 1900, 1904, 1907, 1908, 1911, 1912, 1914, 1923, 1925, 1927, 1931, 1933, 1937, 1951, 1954, 1965, 1967, 1969, 1971, 1972, 1974, 1975, 1977, 1980, 1985, 1988, 1989, 1995, 2001, 2004, 2005, 2007, 2011, 2013 – and now, welcome 2017. Celtic and the Scottish Cup are totally and irredeemably in love with each other. They are like an old married couple, in that they have the odd falling out now and again, but no one can doubt their basic feelings for each other.

And the celebrations on the field! They came and showed us the lovely silver trophy, and the thing was that the players were as entranced and excited by the support, as we were by them. Brendan Rodgers started conducting the choir when it told him that he was going to be here for ten in a row. He had been brought up a Celt, but he had never experienced anything like this, nor could be have dreamed that he would achieve what he did; Kieran Tierney, injured and just back from hospital for the celebrations, lifted the trophy vigorously and kissed the jersey with a passion. He was the boy who was simply living the dream. Others, not perhaps brought up as Celts in places like Edinburgh, Inverness, Sweden, Belgium and the Ivory Coast, were now as committed to the cause as anyone else. It was indeed 'the greatest show on earth'!

Heading back to the buses down Aitkenhead Road, the army moved singing, chanting, clapping, jumping on each other's backs. It was all green and white, but a family of Aberdeen fans stood at the side trying to be inconspicuous and maybe even afraid to cross the mass of Celtic fans. 'Magnanimity in victory,' I had once heard, so I shook their hands and wished them all the best, saying that their day would come. They were a decent bunch of ma, pa and the weans, or as they would have said up there, 'mither, faither, the loon and the quine,' and they were grateful

Celtic with the Scottish Cup.

Brendan Rodgers with the Scottish Cup.

for my words of consolation. Some Celtic fans jeered at me for my kindness, and I am prepared to admit that the Dons would have been unbearable if they had won, but that family was a decent one and they now had a long painful journey back home...and, in the past, we had been there ourselves.

The bus home was uproarious and happy with songs about volunteers approaching border towns, a young man giving his young life high upon the gallows tree, another being gunned down on his way to the Gaelic ground mingled with ten in a row and he's oh, so wonderful as well as the repetitive but compelling champions again oh, eh, oh, eh. We talked about Patrick Roberts and how it was worth breaking the bank to sign him. That inevitably brought up the subject of money, but one fan, in a memorable anti-materialistic, anti-capitalist aphorism, jerked his thumb back in the direction of Glasgow and Hampden and said, 'Money! Money! Money couldna buy a day like that!'

CHAPTER **FOURTEEN**
REFLECTIONS AND COMPARISONS

Well, who would have thought it? 2016/17 was the season we were warned about. Not only would there still be a strong Aberdeen and a new Hearts, it would also be the season in which Rangers would return. Call them Sevco or Newco if you like, but with their red, white and blue, Union Jacks and offensive and nowadays quite ridiculous songs, they looked awfully like the old Rangers to me. Celtic, we were assured, with a new Manager, would have their work cut out to hold their own.

So how did Celtic do it? Well, their new and fresh Manager had, in the first place, the wholehearted backing of the supporters, which frankly Ronnie Deila could not rely upon, certainly towards the end of his reign. This was important. Brendan Rodgers also made two very important signings in Scott Sinclair and Moussa Dembele. It would be a fair bet that not very many Celtic fans had ever heard of either of these two, but they very soon adapted to what was required of them. It was a definite plus that they were both level-headed young men as well, and did not bring any baggage with them, even though Sinclair certainly had cause to be bitter about the way that he had been treated in England.

When new players come into Celtic, it is not easy for them. Whether it was Brendan's good judgement or simply luck, we will never know, but certainly they did very well in contrast to quite a few others in the past – Boerrigter, Pukki, Scepovic, Berget for example – who may have been good players with other clubs and in other countries, but simply did not make it with Celtic. Once again, we realise that Celtic are indeed a unique club. But Dembele and Sinclair, crucially, made an early breakthrough and maintained it!

It also has to be stressed, however, that summer 2016 was by no means a low point in Celtic's history. Far too often did one hear words like 'disaster' being thrown about in the context of Deila by punters who did not really know what 'disaster' meant. John Barnes was a disaster; Tony Mowbray was a disaster; the Kelly regimes of long ago were disasters. Ronnie Deila won the Scottish League for two years in a row! No one will deny that Brendan Rodgers was and remains a far better Manager than Ronnie Deila, but he did start from a reasonably high base line.

Good players were already there. Rodgers' claim to fame was that he made them a great deal better. James Forrest, Stuart Armstrong, Callum McGregor and maybe even Scott Brown came on by leaps and bounds, while the mighty talents of Kieran Tierney were developed. Stefan Johansen the star of 2015 but the flop of 2016 was allowed to leave without any great resistance being shown, while the precocious Patrick Roberts, sadly still merely on loan from Manchester City, was nursed along with a particular emphasis on getting him to use his right foot a little more effectively.

There were other things that were worked on as well. Deila's much vaunted fitness regime had not produced the goods to the extent that the team demanded, and a new effort was made to produce a cadre of perfectly fit young athletes who would be as fast and as enthusiastic in the 89th minute as they had been in the first. There was no excuse for Celtic players not being fit, and hard though the *Daily Record* and other rags would have tried, no stories – certainly no credible or authenticated stories – ever emerged about any drunken misbehaviour or anything like that.

A feature of the season was the amount of times that non-specialist goal scorers – midfielders like Armstrong, McGregor and Rogic – scored from outside the box. It happened so often, and won so many games that it could not have been an accident. This aspect of the game must have been worked on at Lennoxtown. Previous teams had tried rather too often to walk the ball into the net, as if that were the only way to score.

There was a healthy rivalry between Griffiths and Dembele for the 'striker' spot. Both of them had spells out injured, and sometimes both were out, but Rodgers was bright enough not to let either of them become complacent. A place in this team had to be deserved. It could not be taken for granted.

Generally, the team played a good passing game. Very seldom was the ball given away to the opposition. Efe Ambrose, that lovable but accident-prone defender, was a man of the past, and Emilio Izaguirre, admirable man though he was, had now lost out to Kieran Tierney, although Emilio was deployed with credit when Kieran was injured. And it was a better and more disciplined Emilio as well. His annoying habit of charging up the wing beating several men in the process and then blasting wildly across the penalty box on a wing and a prayer had now gone. Mikael Lustig had a few poor games, particularly at the start of the season, but developed splendidly throughout the season into a very mature and confident player with rabonas and the ability now and again to turn on a sixpence and score. He was also a brilliant deputy skipper when Scott Brown was missing.

Normally Celtic teams who score freely also lose soft goals at the back. The Lisbon Lions, for example, often won games by scores like 6–2 or 5–2 because goals were conceded through the concentration on attack. Brendan Rodgers managed to score goals without conceding too many. It took a while before Jozo Simunovich and Dedryck Boyata coalesced as the central defensive pairing. At the beginning of the season, Eoghan O'Connell, Kolo Toure and Erik Sviatchenko had been in contention, and there was little wrong with any of the three of them (Toure was perhaps ageing), but it was Jozo Simunovich and Dedryck Boyata who finished the season imperiously, playing with great authority and co-ordinated teamwork and conceding very few goals.

Boyata suddenly appeared after the New Year and had the added advantage of being able to score goals with his head like Billy McNeill used to do long ago. From forgotten man, he moved to having a song sung about him, about how we no longer had Jason Denayer, 'but it doesn't matter, cos we've got Boyata'.

Craig Gordon retained his reputation as the best shot-stopper around. His kicking remained dubious on occasion, but he radiated confidence and command. He lost his place to Dorus de Vries for a while but soon regained it. He also regained his Scotland place.

The midfield was, of course, the engine of the team. We have mentioned their goal scoring ability but that is not their main function. Their main function is ball winning, control and distribution. And there were loads of them! Ryan Christie, Liam Henderson, Nir Bitton, Tommy Rogic, James Forrest are all excellent players who would have earned a place in most Celtic teams. They could not be guaranteed a place in this one, but when they played they did not let anyone down.

Scott Brown remained inspirational. Never very far from the action, and sometimes closer to it than was wise, as evidenced by his repeated ability to pick up yellow cards, Scott was immense in midfield, and many times we reflected on just what a good signing he had been for Gordon Strachan all those years ago. He plays, as they say, with his heart on his sleeve.

Brendan Rodgers probably realised from an early stage that a squad with this talent did not need to be coached so much as encouraged and told how good they were. His first early achievement was qualifying them for the sectional stages of the Champions League (all right, it was tight but he managed it!) and then by the middle of September he had defeated his three main domestic challengers in Hearts, Aberdeen and Rangers, so confidence was high and Brendan kept it high. Europe saw two serious reverses. The 7–0 scoreline in Barcelona cannot be described as anything other than a hammering, but there was no collateral damage in Scotland. The worst performance of the season was that curious, timid performance against Borussia Monchengladbach at Parkhead. We had Rangers the following Sunday in a Scottish League Cup semi-final and we feared the worst. Not a bit of it. Brendan rallied the troops and we won.

Celtic went on to the field for most games expecting to win – and duly did. The big challenge for Rodgers in the future will be to persuade his players to take the field in European games expecting to win. Home games will have the major advantage of the best fans in the world (in this context of lifting their team) but away games will be a great deal trickier. The verdict of history has still to be delivered on Brendan Rodgers, but he is off to a good start. The fans love him, but it must be stressed that they have not yet been put to the test. If we hit a bad spell, the fans must stick by him!

The confidence that Rodgers brought had its effect on the other challengers.

Hearts, suffering from major problems in the boardroom and the perceived difficulty of Managers working there, collapsed woefully after their opening day defeat by Celtic and were never really in the race for any trophy. Aberdeen, efficiently run at board level and with a dedicated and committed Manager in Derek McInnes, possibly missed their best opportunity to win the League in 2016, particularly after they beat Deila's rocky Celtic in February of that year, but they had the fatal tendency to blow up at home in 2016, and to an extent that happened in 2017 as well. Nevertheless, they had some good players and the fact that they finished second in all three competitions does say something in their favour. They did win the League Cup in 2014, beating Inverness in a penalty shoot-out, but that is their only trophy this century. Losing heavily to Celtic as early as August in 2016/17 probably told them that they were good, but not good enough to beat Celtic. They believed that.

And what about Rangers? They were still emerging from the lower reaches of the Leagues, and for them the key match was 10 September at Parkhead. If they had won that one, things might have been different for them, but they lost 1–5. They never recovered from that, and in the spring they sacked their diligent but ineffective Manager Mark Warburton, a man who came across tolerably well in interviews and with whom one could imagine oneself having a friendly argument with in a pub or a café. A nice man but manifestly not up to the demands of that job. He was not nearly nasty enough.

With Rangers psyched out and still with their death wish, there was hardly anyone else. Partick Thistle, St Johnstone, Ross County, Inverness and Dundee all put up a good show when Celtic played them, but everyone expected and even knew that Celtic were going to win the League. Such was the mesmeric hold that Rodgers and Celtic held upon Scotland in season 2016/17.

So how good were they, these 'Invincibles'? In a sense, this is a foolish question to ask because all we can really say is that they were far too good for anything else that was put in front of them at this point. They failed (and failed badly, if we are to be honest about it) in Europe even though we had a couple of good games against Manchester City, so they are immediately not as good as the Lisbon Lions – not that anyone would have dared to suggest that anyway, but they were still 'pretty good'. But how good?

To take the League record first. Thirty-four wins out of thirty-eight with only four draws is more than totally acceptable. It is, indeed, unparalleled in modern times, and we really have to go back 120 years before we come close to equalling it. In the first place, let us concede that in 1898/99 Rangers had a 100 per cent League record. They did have a good side – it was their first of four in a row under a talented Manager called William Wilton – but Celtic were not all that far behind them either and did beat them in the Scottish Cup Final 2–0, and also lifted the Glasgow Charity Cup that year. And, of course, the big difference between 1899 and 2017 lay in the Scottish League itself. It consisted of only ten clubs, they played eighteen games and in public opinion, it had nothing like the 'clout' that it does now, far inferior, in public perception, to the 'Blue Riband' as they called the Scottish Cup. So, having conceded that Rangers were good in 1899, what about Celtic the year before?

1897/98 was a remarkable season for the club. They emerged from a 'car crash' (or possibly, 'horse and cart crash' might be more appropriate imagery for Victorian Scotland) of a season in 1896/97 which had seen a player revolt and a humiliating Scottish Cup exit to Arthurlie. They reacted by appointing a new Manager in April 1897, the energetic, knowledgeable, genial and charming Willie Maley, and won the Scottish League, winning fifteen games and drawing three. They were a fine side with men like Dan Doyle, Sandy McMahon and Johnny Campbell all in their prime. They set down a marker at the end of September 1897 with a 4–0 win over Rangers at Ibrox, and a feature of the season was great goal scoring with neighbours Clyde being the chief whipping boys to the tune of 6–1 at Celtic Park early in the season and then 9–1 on Barrowfield Park on Christmas Day. Partick Thistle were on the receiving end of six as well, and the only draws were all 0–0 – at Tynecastle in September, an odd game at St Mirren a month later and then against Rangers at Parkhead when the League was well won, the

New Year's Day game having had to be abandoned because of constant crowd problems of overcrowding rather than disorder.

The League was won in the second-to-last game on 12 February as Celtic beat St Mirren 3–0 at Parkhead, while 100 miles away at Carolina Port, Dundee, Barney Battles played his part. Barney was once of Parkhead but he was one of the mutineers of November 1896. Along with two others, he refused to take the field because of the presence of a certain journalist in the Press Box. He was suspended and moved on for that, but was now repentant and plying his reluctant trade with Dundee. On this occasion, he did his real love a great service by scoring a late goal to beat Rangers. A precursor to Albert Kidd, eighty-eight years later! And Barney would soon return to the fold.

Celtic thus won the League for the fourth time, and won it well, going, as we say, undefeated through the League programme. But they were not undefeated in other competitions. In particular, they exited the Scottish Cup in January to Third Lanark at Cathkin Park, in a 2–3 defeat which cannot entirely be explained away by the absence through injury of the talismanic Sandy McMahon, who had hurt himself at Dundee the previous week. Not only that, but they lost to Rangers in the

Celtic in 1898. Look at Willie Maley's headgear!

Glasgow Cup after two replays (and yes, people asked the obvious question about that!) and then in the Glasgow Charity Cup as well.

So, 1897/98, although an honourable year for the club, cannot really be rated in the same bracket at 2016/17. We should be proud of their achievement in the League that season, but Maley had not yet reached the apex of his talents. That would happen ten years later and his best season was, without any shadow of a doubt, 1907/08.

This team was, until 1967, considered to be the best of them all. Every Celtic youngster heard their father or grandfather going round the house saying Adams, McNair and Weir; Young, Loney and Hay; Bennett, McMenemy, Quinn, Somers and Hamilton. So where were the weak links in that line-up? There weren't any, and with Eck McNair, Sunny Jim Young, Jimmy Napoleon McMenemy and Jimmy Quinn on board, Celtic were going to win trophies.

They did. They swept the boards, winning everything that was asked of them – the Scottish Cup, the Scottish League, the Glasgow Cup and the Glasgow Charity Cup! Such a pity there was no European or even British dimension in those days.

'He made them the greatest of them all.' Celtic in 1908.

They would have won them as well, and oh, how we must envy those supporters of 110 years ago who could enjoy such talent!

And yet, they were not 'invincible'. They lost three times in the League, all away from home to Aberdeen, Hearts and Dundee, and they had their fair share of draws as well. The League was much expanded by that time to eighteen teams and thirty-four games, but this team won it comfortably. So there were blemishes in 1908, but they tend to be ignored by historians, for the team was such a great one.

Two other seasons in which Celtic won every competition that they entered were 1915/16 and 1916/17. Unfortunately, these seasons must be immediately qualified by the statement that they were in the middle of that dreadful war, and apart from anything else, there was no Scottish Cup. It was a strange decision to cancel the trophy in some ways, for the Scottish League was able to function, albeit with many problems. We also have to acknowledge that wartime football was a haphazard business, with not every club able to field its best team, so 1915/16 and 1916/17, although triumphant for Celtic, are incomplete without the Scottish Cup. In any case, neither of these seasons was totally unflawed. The team went from 13 November 1915 until 21 April 1917 undefeated, but this statistic, impressive though it is, means that a League game was lost in each season. Indeed, before the defeat to Hearts in November 1915, Celtic had also lost to Rangers and St Mirren.

It must be emphasised that this is not to disparage or denigrate the great Celtic teams of those difficult years. Indeed, they deserve all the more credit for what they did to raise morale in those terrible times. People always need something to be happy about. In the midst of so many other cataclysmic events in Europe, the high seas, Turkey, Mesopotamia and even, very poignantly, Ireland, they found some solace at Celtic Park.

Had this war not come along, there were already signs in 1914 that a great Celtic team was developing. The Scottish League, Scottish Cup and Glasgow Charity Cup were annexed, they set up a record by not conceding a goal between 13 December 1913 and 28 February 1914 – and there was the great Patsy Gallacher in his prime (and playing in the same team as Jimmy Napoleon McMenemy – wow!) but 1913/14 cannot really be considered in the same breath as 2016/17 because a poor performance in October 1913 against Third Lanark lost the Glasgow Cup.

So, what about the other three treble winning seasons? The treble was, of course, only possible in Scotland since the Second World War, when the Scottish League Cup arrived on the scene. Celtic won the treble in 1967, 1969 and 2001. We must at this point put up our hand and acknowledge that Rangers have done it oftener in 1949, 1964, 1976, 1978, 1993, 1999 and 2003 – but in each of these seasons there was something a great deal wrong at a dysfunctional Celtic Park! Jock Stein, for example, was out injured in a car crash for 1975/76 and lapsed into a sort of catatonic depression after the sale of Kenny Dalglish in 1977/78, while Martin O'Neill was too preoccupied with Europe in 2002/03 and on several occasions took his eye off the domestic ball.

It is hard to say very much against the 1967 team. Their record speaks for itself, and it is the opinion of many detached and unbiased English commentators, notably Sam Leitch and Kenneth Wolstenholme, that they were the best of them all. There was not a single weakness in the team, and they had the advantage of being great entertainers as well with loads of goals and beautiful passing football. And yet they were not 'invincible'. They reached Hogmanay 1966 without being defeated, but then went down to a good Dundee United team on New Year's Eve. Someone had to beat them sometime we felt, and indeed they were maybe lucky to get off with a draw at Pittodrie the week before.

They also lost to Dundee United at Parkhead in strange circumstances. It was the Wednesday after they had won the Scottish Cup on the Saturday, and they would have won the Scottish League if they beat Dundee United. But they lost. The widely held belief in certain sections of the support that it was all 'set up' so that Celtic could win the League at Ibrox on the Saturday is almost certainly fanciful, and all that the exhausted Celts were guilty of was a little complacency and taking the foot off the pedal. In any case, they won the League with a draw in the Ibrox rain on the Saturday, so it didn't really matter, but the two defeats by the Tannadice men are a small blemish for the pedants to pick up on.

The treble winners of 1969 were almost as good. It was certainly my opinion that the football played in the spring (in particular the two Cup Finals in April, 6–2 v. Hibs in the League Cup and 4–0 v. Rangers in the Scottish Cup) was even better than that played in 1967 – an ambitious claim, certainly, but watch YouTube for the Hibs League Cup Final if you don't believe me! But that came in the wake of a heart breaking exit from Europe after a bad defensive error against AC Milan. In any case, this great side managed to lose twice to Rangers, unluckily on both occasions admittedly, in the Scottish League, and had three insipid draws on hard grounds in December against Falkirk, Kilmarnock and Airdrie, leading the weaker brethren to believe some of the newspaper crap that they were 'on the slide' in a rather weak joke about frosty pitches. They then blew up spectacularly against Greenock Morton at Parkhead in the night that all three trophies were driven round the running track on top of a car! The trophy display was the highlight of that particular night, for the players forgot they were expected to continue their superhuman activities! But I am being very critical. 1969 was also a very good season indeed.

And then we come to the most recent of all the trebles – 2001, and the apogee of Henrik Larsson and others of that exceptionally fine side of Martin O'Neill. Once again, some great football with consistently unbeatable form round about the turn of the year – 6–0 against Aberdeen and Kilmarnock, 4–0 at Tannadice against Dundee United, for example – but the big problem with this season was Europe (not for the first nor last time) and a big, dirty and rather inexplicable 1–5 hammering at Ibrox in November. No one saw that one coming, and when the following game was a poor 0–0 at Easter Road, we began to wonder. In the game after that, Dunfermline scored first, but the team rallied to win and from then on never looked back on their way to the treble, although there was once again a little 'foot off the pedal' behaviour and defeats from Dundee and Kilmarnock after the League was won. Once again, I feel I will incur the charge of excessive criticism of what was a very fine side and without any shadow of doubt the best team since the Jock Stein era.

How many jerseys does he need? Leigh Griffiths has at least two here?

So, having established that there is not really a perfect 100 per cent season – indeed, such an occurrence would say a great deal about the rest of Scottish football – where does all this place 2016/17? Taking everything into account and allowing for the standard of opposition and other things, I would place 2016/17 fourth in the best Celtic seasons of them all. First simply has to be 1966/67; second is 1907/08 (because an old supporter whom I talked to on a bus once, and who had had the privilege of seeing both 1908 and 1967, said, when pressed about who was better, after a long pause of considered reflection, 'I widna like to say, leddie'); third is 1968/69; and then comes 2016/17, with 1968/69 just edging it because the exit from Europe was narrow and unfortunate to AC Milan (the eventual winners) whereas 2016/17 saw a 7–0 defeat at the Nou Camp which was embarrassing. 2000/01 with that 1–5 defeat at Ibrox comes fifth.

The 'invincible' season is thus well up there, and the potential for the future to do even better is still there. Interesting (is it not?) that many great teams and many great players – Patsy Gallacher, Jimmy McGrory, Jimmy Delaney, to name but three – never featured in any of the superbly great seasons. This is not to denigrate them. Rather, it emphasises (does it not?) just how good a season 2016/17 was. How will history judge it in fifty years' time?

One hopes, of course, that they will say it was the first of many, and not quite as good as the side which won the Champions League in 2020 and...now, now, don't be cynical or pessimistic! Believe!

24040259R00111

Printed in Great Britain
by Amazon